The Ill Tempered String Quartet

The Ill Tempered String Quartet

A *Vademecum for the Amateur Musician*

by
Lester Chafetz

McFarland & Company, Inc., Publishers
Jefferson, North Carolina, and London

I would be remiss if I did not acknowledge the indispensable
contributions of my many chamber music companions,
who provided not only many of the anecdotes employed
but the experience that made this book possible.
Particular gratitude is expressed to Robert P. Cahn
of Millburn, New Jersey, with whom I played
in quartets most often. Bob neutralized bad temper
with good humor and fine musicianship.

British Library Cataloguing-in-Publication data available

Library of Congress Cataloguing-in-Publication Data

Chafetz, Lester, 1929–
The ill tempered string quartet.

Musicography: p. 95.
Includes index.
1. Music in the home.
2. String quartet.
I. Title.
ML67.C5   1989   785′.06′8   88-27354

ISBN 0-89950-398-5 (lib. bdg.; 50# acid-free natural paper) ⊗

Manufactured in the United States of America

McFarland   Box 611   Jefferson NC 28640

Dedicated
with love and gratitude
to my wife, Jan, for all her support
in this effort and her amused tolerance
over many years of my idiosyncrasies,
only some of which may be inferred
from this text.

Foreword

It was very uncomfortable. I was 12 years old. I felt my mother staring at me, and I looked up from the book I was reading to ask if something was wrong. "You're a bum," she said. (She was an astute judge of character.) "All you do all day is sit around reading. Go out and get a job." I started working part-time soon after. Decades later, with the expectation that my children would be graduated from college and off my payroll, I took early retirement from my job in pharmaceutical research and development. I bought a computer, had business cards printed that represented me as "Associates," and went to my office at home each day to read, write scientific papers and listen to music. I had been playing in a weekly amateur string quartet for several years by that time, and one of many unfinished manuscripts I had was the one that became this book.

In the beginning I had plenty of time in which to focus on my writings. The music manuscript was recreation from scientific work, just as the chamber music sessions provided recreation from my work. Recreation is not relaxation. Success in my profession came much faster and easier than competence in quartet playing. I had begun writing about my stressful string-playing with no intention of publishing the writings. It was catharsis, and the humor in it was ego-defense. This manuscript developed rapidly to the point where I had enough written to interest the publisher. Just after this happened, my leisure time was eroded. First, in spite of my diffident efforts at self-promotion, my consulting calendar became crowded. Then, with the encouragement of my wife, who never could get used to having me in the house on weekdays, I found a job as a professor. Finishing the book was accomplished when I was once again out of the house on weekdays. It began as a labor of love, finishing it was a lovely release from a self-imposed obligation. My wife complained, "I can't win. If I don't ask how the book is coming, you say I am not interested. If I do ask, you accuse me of nagging." This, then, is the origin of this book.

I cannot remember a close relative who owned a piano when I was a child. People with parlor pianos were a couple of economic and cultural classes above us. There were 21 of us cousins, children of my mother and her brother and five sisters. Violin-playing was much admired. My father had been a self-taught violinist, and my oldest brother showed aptitude. Parents in the wider family who could coerce their children to violin lessons were spared both the expense of purchase and the bother of selecting an instrument. Every family had at least one "Bohemian Strad" in a closet; often a ¾ size and a full size. The relatives were happy to lend these, motivated both by family generosity and the desire to get out of sight a reminder of the failure of one or more of their own children to seize the opportunity to have become a world-famous virtuoso.

All these instruments resembled from a distance the violins played by Heifetz, Elman and Kreisler, but every one of them produced thin and querulous tone. A complaint about their sound invariably brought forth the reproof, "Heifetz can make a cigar box sound like a Sradivarius." Perhaps this was so, but we, with the talent for making a Stradivarius sound like a cigar box, needed the help of a good fiddle more than did Heifetz. I have a dim memory of my father revarnishing one of these violins in hope that he could rediscover the Secret of Cremona. He was disappointed, but he did no harm.

In my immediate family, only the second brother, my "brother-the-artist," refused violin lessons. (When this gifted anomaly was in art school, my mother and I encountered the mother of one of is high-school classmates on the street one day. When told my brother aspired to be an artist, she exploded, "Artist, Schmartist. Dere are only t'ree t'ings; a doc-tuh, a law-yuh or an eye-petition!") Graphic arts got little respect, but everyone in our circle admired violinists and valued learning.

My father never missed a radio performance of classical music, and he insisted on quiet when we listened. He took me to a performance in the last concert tour of Fritz Kreisler, and I realized much later that it took a significant portion of his resources to do it. I was a disappointment to him in my progress as a violin student. The last years of his life and my stay in high school coincided. I played only outside my home, in the school orchestra where I occupied second chair in the first violins. One of my friends characterized my status as, "second sour note from the right."

I dropped from the ranks of amateur players for several years. As a starveling graduate student at the University of Wisconsin, I was able to afford the recitals of the Pro Arte String Quartet. They were fine musicians, they were wide-ranging in repertory — and their recitals were free. (The status of a graduate student at a great university is one of very few in life in which poverty is respected and carries privileges.) Familiarity with the enormous range of chamber music provided by the artists-in-residence developed in me a devotion to that medium. From then on, I was a subscriber to chamber music series.

Much later in my career, I started playing violin again. I played through the violin parts of concertos and sonatas by myself, skipping the passages that were difficult. In retrospect, I played small percentages of the total notes in these. If one were willing to overlook my weakness in rhythmic sense, there were only two things wrong with my playing, my bow arm and my left hand. Eventually my efforts led to playing violin in a quartet at home. The psychological aberration in which we hear what we are trying to play instead of what we play in actuality is mentioned in this text. Without it, no beginner would have courage to continue. The complement of one of the earliest manifestations of the ITSQ included another violinist with more experience than I. He knew several second violin parts, leaving me exposed in my inadequacies as first violin. My reach far exceeded my grasp. The quartet was faced with a crisis when my playing and manner alienated our viola player permanently. No other viola player at our level was available on a weekly basis. In response, I obtained a viola. It required very little time to develop equal incompetence on both instruments. Finding an excellent first violin willing to play with us gave me an easier part and an opportunity to learn ensemble. Realization of my technical deficiencies led to violin lessons from a good teacher. Improvement was rapid, and the lessons provided a foundation for analysis and solution of technical problems that came later.

Chamber music originated as music for amateur players, but

composition of it requires the best ideas composers can put forth. A lack of inspiration cannot be hidden by orchestral color effects. The economy of means, one player to a part, brings out the best inspirations of the composers and exposes the contribution of each of the players. Attempting to recreate these magnificent inspirations of great genius for oneself is a challenge. Succeeding in the attempt, expecially after failures, provides a thrill of accomplishment. It may take years to achieve the goal of playing chamber music well, and the goal may not be hit on every try. The effort required obliterates all other concerns, making it nearly perfect recreation. In truth, the goal is never achieved, because we move it further ahead with each leap in ability. Jerry Della Femina wrote about his advertising profession that it was more fun than anything else people could do with clothes on. We amateur chamber music players can steal that description for our sessions.

Table of Contents

TABLE OF CONTENTS

Introduction

This book is intended for amateur string instrument players who want to play string quartets and other forms of chamber music. The writer perceives a need by amateurs of instruction in the recruitment of players, the physical arrangements of quartet sessions, the literature, the lore, the proprieties and the sociopathology of string quartet players and their families. It is the book the writer would have liked to have available when he began playing chamber music several years ago.

It may be considered presumptuous for an amateur musician to essay a serious book on a venerable and venerated art. One would rightly decry the arrogance of an amateur tennis player or golfer who writes a manual on the technique of hitting a ball, and this writer will leave technical instruction on fiddle playing to those with professional qualifications. Several fine books and articles have been published on playing string quartets, nearly all of them by professional musicians. About 50 years ago, Aulich and Heimeran, German amateur players, wrote a book titled, *Das stillvergnügte Streichquartett*, which might be translated, "the well-adjusted string quartet." The publisher of the English edition used the title *The Well Tempered String Quartet*, a play on Bach's "Well Tempered Clavier." Although the authors were amateurs, they wrote about their own long established foursome, described their sessions as rehearsals and their goal as performances for friends and acquaintances. (How many friends were downgraded to acquaintances by these performance programs was left unrecorded.) In contrast, the locally notorious Ill Tempered String Quartet — of which this writer was a founding member — comprised a list of 20 people in any one year, of whom four were assembled at short notice. They do not rehearse, they do not perform; they play. If the ITSQ has an audience, the auditors are incidental, usually consisting of the host's tone deaf (or stone deaf) relative or a friend who is interested in esoteric behavior patterns. The ITSQ ignores such auditors, conceding to their presence only in providing free access to the host's liquor cabinet and suggesting they come equipped with reading material or a handicraft project.

Why the "ill tempered" descriptor in the title? Displays of bad temper are not uncommon among amateur chamber music players, deriving from frustration at inability to count, to articulate the notes seen on the page (and heard in the mind) on the instrument and to achieve a balance in dynamics. The emotion is analogous to that of an amateur golfer who knows that the standard of the professional in his sport is unattainable but keeps trying to raise his own level of competence to respectability, to a level where better players will accept him. It has been well said that anything worth doing is worth doing badly, but it is easier on the ego and less damaging to the psyche to be at the same level of competence as one's companions. An ill tempered string quartet is better than no shared music at all, but its aim should be to raise its competence to the point where it no longer deserves its name.

Why "string quartet" in the name? The string quartet, two violins, one viola and one cello—the names of the instruments are applied also to their players and the parts they play—became a standard form of expression for composers more than 200 years ago. Haydn is credited with more than 75 compositions for this group, Mozart with 24, Beethoven with 17, Schubert with 15, Schumann 3, Mendelssohn 7, Bartók 6, Prokofiev 2 and Shostakovich 15, to give a quick sampling encompassing two centuries. The literature for other numbers and combinations of instruments is much smaller; string duos, trios and quintets will, however, not be ignored, nor will music for strings with piano and other "hetero" instruments.

A definition for chamber music is music played by more than two and fewer than ten players. Its essential feature is that each player has his own part. It might be argued that two players constitute a chamber group, and the definition might be qualified with the requirement that at least half the number of players must be string instruments; however, a sonata for any instrument and piano has the character of chamber music. An amateur string instrument player might find satisfaction in playing in an orchestra instead of or in addition to playing chamber music. There are many such people. There is a vast difference between chamber music and an orchestra for a string instrument player. An orchestra violinist may be one of twelve or more first violins or second violins, because many string instruments are needed to balance the volume of sound emitted by few wind instruments. Some string instrument players enjoy being part of a choir of strings, a part of the huge instrument "played" by a conductor. For the chamber music purist, however, the chief value of amateur symphony orchestras is that their personnel lists can be raided for potential chamber music companions. Suffice it to record that the satisfactions are different.

We live in an age where music schools graduate many times the number of wonderful instrumental players than there are positions available as soloists, recitalists, in orchestras and in chamber groups. Standards of professional music performance approach perfection. Every community now has the opportunity to hear music of superlative standard in live performances, and technology allows us to listen to recorded performances by great artists at home and in our automobiles. Why not relax and listen instead of trying to play the music oneself? One could extend this to ask why there are amateur painters, tennis players, bowlers or card players. The answer lies in the word *amateur*, derived from the word "to love." There is a joy in being able to get through, however badly, a masterpiece like a late Beethoven quartet that is as great or greater than hearing the same work performed by one of the marvelous professional groups, and the inside knowledge of its structure gained from performing a part — or trying — heightens the amateur's appreciation of the professional. The amateur provides the informed audience for the professional, the mass market for concert tickets, music lessons, books and magazines on music, instruments and published music parts. Professional musicians could no more exist without amateur musicians than could tennis or golf tournaments without their amateurs as consumers.

There is great intellectual gratification just in sitting down at home to play a Haydn string quartet published 200 years ago, using instruments hardly different than those established in form nearly 400 years — and there is a rueful realization that the performances 200 years past may well have been better. (For a quartet composed of poor or inexperienced players, more of the satisfaction is intellectual than sensory, but domestic chamber music playing is satisfying at many levels.) At the time of Haydn (1732–1809), chamber music was written mostly for performance by amateurs. Haydn's contemporary, Thomas Jefferson, was an amateur chamber music player, and a visitor to his home at Monticello in Virginia is shown the folding string quartet stand among his inventions. Benjamin Franklin wrote a string quartet for violins and cello. Mozart dedicated three quartets with prominent cello parts to King Friedrich Wilhelm II of Prussia, reputedly a better cellist than a king. The Prince of Wales who became George IV was praised for his cello playing by Haydn during the composer's visit to England in 1791. Examples of chamber music players among people prominent by reason of birth or accomplishment in fields other than music are numerous. We who play chamber music carry on a long and honorable tradition. This book is written for those who are interested in getting started in amateur chamber music as a leisure activity and those established in it who might find it interesting in comparison with their own experiences. It might also prove expository for friends and families of amateur chamber music players. Finally, amateur chamber music playing is a serious endeavor, but serious does not mean grim. It is hoped the reader may find some entertainment along with the instruction.

I. How Many Players in a String Quartet?

Any fool knows that a string quartet means a group comprising two violinists, a violist and a cellist. Any amateur who is not a fool recognizes soon that a regular weekly quartet session needs a far bigger list. A nice round number is 20, of whom about half should be cellists (unless the would-be quartet player is one). Amateur instrumentalists have career and family obligations. A business trip, a dance recital by someone's ungrateful (and ungraceful) daughter, a theater or concert subscription, a planned vacation, orchestra rehearsals, a prior call from a quartet host who promises more skillful players or a better refreshment table, or some other activity might be given priority over your evening. Regular quartet playing demands a degree of adaptability. Of course, there are amateur quartets who maintain the same complement of players for several years, meeting regularly, knowing who will play what part, and deciding beforehand what will be played. These are not the principal recipients of the sagacious counsel offered here. Inevitably, however, there comes a time when one of the stalwarts of even such a quartet has the bad grace to drop out by reason of job transfer, accident, illness or death. Then comes the necessity to recruit players.

The Impresario

It is the host who invites the players, and only he has the certainty of playing. For this reason, this work is written from the viewpoint of the host. The host takes care of the logistics of time and place and has the responsibility of inviting the players, providing the necessary physical arrangements and providing refreshment to the players; however, this is more than counterbalanced by the opportunity to play and elimination of travel time to the session. Some players, by reason of their domestic situation, are unable to be hosts often or at all, and they must depend on their playing skill and pleasant personality for invitations. It follows logically that a poor player with uncongenial personality must volunteer to be host often to get playing experience. (With increasing experience and competence, a major source of stress is diminished, and a curmudgeon may reveal charm. One does well not to proscribe anyone permanently.) It has been said that good judgment derives from experience — and experience comes from bad judgment. It should be noted, too, that improvement in playing chamber music, like other forms of learning, occurs in quanta, discrete leaps in ability, not as a continuum. Taking lessons on the technique of one's instrument eases the process. Playing experience helps in reading music and establishing ensemble, but it does not help executive ability; directed practice does.

The ACMP

An incomparable organization called The Amateur Chamber Music Players, Inc. (ACMP) was founded in 1946 on the initiative of Leonard A. Strauss, an Indianapolis business executive who wanted to spend his evenings at something more satisfying than playing his violin alone in his hotel room when on trips. It has grown since under the guidance of a dedicated few lovers — literally, "amateurs" — of chamber music, most notably the late Helen Rice. Its primary function is to publish a list of players by state and province for North America every two years and an Overseas Directory on alternate years. (The 1988–9 Directory is touted to contain names of "members in the United States, Canada, Mexico, Central America and adjacent islands." In an earlier Directory, a listing was provided for a clarinet player in Guam — a rather long sail from the mainland.)

Members of the ACMP, who make whatever annual contribution they can — there are gentle guidelines offered but no set dues — provide their names, the instruments they play, a code letter for their proficiency, their business and home addresses and telephone numbers, their availability during the week, and, with married women, their maiden names to aid in identification. (Not all women provide this information. Nowadays, the popularity of multiple—successive, that is—marriages and of the use of maiden names professionally may confound such listings.) ACMP proficiency ratings are "Pro" for professional, "A" for excellent, "B" good, "C" fair and "D" for "etc." A guide for self-rating, devised by a British volunteer, is provided by ACMP, but it is the player who decides the rating or ratings with his listing. (A player may claim to be a Vl-B, good violinist, and only a Vla-C, fair violist.)

One listed as a "Pro" may be the concertmaster of a major symphony orchestra or someone who gives fiddle lessons to beginners; a "Pro" is anyone who makes money by playing. A fundamental principle for readers of this text should be, *Never let a professional hear you play unless he or she is being paid by you!* Violation of this principle may lead to severe damage to the ego. Spike Hughes, in a preface to a book by Joseph Szigeti, tells of practicing the second violin part of a Haydn quartet with a second violin solo—a good guess is the Op. 74, No. 2—and inviting Szigeti and other professionals to his home for a chamber music evening where he could sit in for this one quartet. Predictably, the attempt ended in disaster.

Self-Rating

Some players qualify their proficiency with + or − signs, but it must be recognized that ratings are subjective and may change with state of practice and health. One Vl-B may be accurate unerringly in keeping time but produce an uncertain intonation and scratchy sound, while another may exceed the reasonable limits of rubato and emit gorgeous tone. A self-assured instrumentalist might call himself A-level, while a better player with a more reticent personality will settle for a "B."

One of the characteristics distinguishing an amateur from a professional in any field—apart from the obvious one that that latter gets paid—is that the amateur is inconsistent in a much wider range. The professional functions in a narrow range between near perfection and unforgettable; the amateur swings between incompetent and excellent. The amateur has his good outings and his bad. Sometimes the poor accountings for himself can be attributed to lack of opportunity for practice, distractions by personal or professional problems, fatigue or other causes. Other times, with all of these negative factors operative, the amateur will rise above them and play at his best. It is inexplicable, and this very inconsistency is a motivating factor. With experience, the amateur is undiscouraged by a poor showing, knowing that he will rise above his normal level of incompetence to shine forth brightly on some other evening. Given this fact of amateur performance, use of + or − signs with a rating is an abuse of the significance even of such a semiquantitative system as A–D.

A beginner is well-advised to find people with similar ratings, perhaps recruiting a tolerant Vl-A or Vl-B as 1st violin, and to experiment only in the company of people he has played with before. The better the other players the more quickly the tyro will improve; good players, however, will want to play with better players, so homeostasis obtains. The ACMP Directory is a good start for finding other players within a convenient area, and those called may provide referrals to other potential players who are not listed. (Some members drop out after having made regular arrangements; other people never bother to join. A pity, because one can think of no other organization that provides so much potential pleasure to its membership and demands so little from them. The 5000 or so listings are likely a small fraction of the number of chamber music players that are available.) Each new quartet companion contributes to the experience of the others, although not necessarily their enjoyment.

Membership in ACMP enables people to find quartet players during their travels, members willing to arrange chamber music sessions being identified by an asterisk in the listing. In addition to the practical uses of the ACMP Directory, it provides nutritious fodder for idle browsing. One can frequently recognize names of people distinguished in fields other than music, a recent example having been a congressman who listed his rating as a violinist, violist and cellist along with his office number in Washington. Scanning the listing for Massachusetts–Boston

Area, for example, one encounters the Appalachian Mountain Club, which offers information on combining outdoor activities (skiing, hiking, etc.) with chamber music. How skillful one must be to schuss down a slope with a cello!

Getting in Experience

Early in his chamber music career, when he was a Vl-D misrepresenting himself as a Vl-C and a Vla for whom the ACMP's "D" rating could be considered an encomium, the writer had a generous impulse during conversation with an acquaintance at work, a Vl-B/Vla-B, who complained that he never had opportunity to play first violin. Having just acquired a viola, the writer set up a quartet evening with the coworker as first violin and himself as a violist. The coworker arrived with a practiced and annotated group of quartets. The tyro violist missed his first entrance and was castigated with a sneer of contempt from the first's chair, undermining his confidence and destroying his executive ability for the entire evening.

After a troubled night, the would-be violist went off to work, where soon he was greeted by the object of his philanthropy. The latter provided a lengthy and scathing critique of the violist's efforts, the unkindest cut being, "People who play quartets like you are like vandals who slash a Rembrandt masterpiece in a museum." Such is the resiliency of the human spirit that after only a couple of weeks the writer retrieved his instruments from their hiding place and returned to the attempt to make music. On close inspection it was found there was no visible damage to the sheet music, and the damage to its composers had been evanescent.

Several months later, after more experience on the viola, the writer set up a repeat of the evening with the same players. This went well, but the writer took the precaution of instructing his secretary and staff that his coworker must be intercepted and denied access to him if he appeared at the office the next day. Notwithstanding this experience, identifying a second violin or viola in an established amateur quartet and inviting that person to be the first violin in a quartet of near beginners can be worthwhile.

Orchestra Lists

Another source of potential quartet companions is the personnel lists of amateur orchestras, available from the orchestra secretary with addresses and telephone numbers. This might be obtained from an acquaintance in the orchestra. Failing this, it may be worthwhile to appear at an initial meeting of the orchestra, sit unobtrusively at the last chair of a string section and importune likely recruits during breaks. (The signal for when to stop attending orchestra rehearsals is either the judgment that players cannot be recruited or a demand for membership dues, whichever comes first. Of course, some people will actually enjoy continuing to play in the orchestra, thereby making themselves unavailable for quartet sessions on the rehearsal evening! There is no accounting for tastes.)

Serendipity

Other expedients are getting referrals from local school or university music faculties, violin repairers and dealers, who are frequently amateur players themselves, and placing advertisements in local papers. (Some years ago, my wife arranged an advertisement in our local paper for a cellist. This was successful. She liked to say afterwards that her husband may not be the only man in the neighborhood who "fiddled around," but he was probably the only one who did so with his mate's assistance.) Serendipity may play a role in finding players. One quartet player recognized that a stranger passing by his office was whistling a theme from a Beethoven quartet. He accosted the whistler, who readily confessed to being a fine violinist with a love for chamber music.

Family Ties

Lucky is the amateur who has a spouse who plays. Sometimes a child will become proficient and fill a gap in arranging a quartet session for a year or so, and there are even instances where a quartet can be constituted from members of the household. More enduring are the "mama and papa" quartet players, many of whom are unequal in their proficiency. They may have met while the one was concertmaster in an orchestra and the other in the seat furthest to the rear, or one may have become a player after marriage. The more proficient of the two sometimes plays on two levels, taking the second violin or viola part in a quartet with excellent players and leading in a session with the less skilled spouse. For the prospective quartet evening host, being able to recruit two players with one call is a coup, and the disparity in their ability is more often a blessing than a problem. Excellent players have little difficulty finding a place in a quartet. Those of lesser experience or ability can have the advantage of playing with a better player than will usually play with them by calling a "mama and papa" of unequal ability.

The number of potential players increases with one's experience in playing quartets, so it may be expected that the recruitment difficulties will ease with time. Of course, this depends on the quality of the experience. Some recruits may decide never to accept another invitation after the first session; others may decide after long trial and travail that a state of irreconcilable musical or personal incompatibility exists. One must keep a healthy mental perspective, refusing to view rejection of a second invitation as a personal affront. The society of chamber music enthusiasts, meeting for the common purpose of trying to make music, like all societies, is founded on mutual agreement.

Invitational Etiquette

Most quartet sessions are arranged by telephone. Although the telephone provides great convenience, it is an intrusive device. A caller has no way of knowing if the person telephoned is busy at that time. Beginning with something like, "I am trying to arrange a quartet session for Wednesday or Thursday evening, and I would like to invite you" wastes no time, and it usually elicits a pleasant response. Calling someone at work is an accepted practice, too. If the recipient is not available, his coworkers will arrange for him to return the call.

Calling a stranger to invite him or her to a quartet session at one's home is usually a pleasant experience. A common interest exists, the desire to play string quartets, and those called are usually flattered by the invitation to play. Rarely, however, a would-be host is faced with an interrogatory. "What music do you play? Whom have you played with? You say you have been playing Mozart's 'Haydn' Quartets, Beethoven Opus 18 and most of Haydn's first two books! Man, don't you know you can spend a lifetime just studying Mozart?" The first two questions should be answered honestly, the third met with, "Thanks for your time. Haydn died for our sins," following immediately with an emphatic bang of the receiver. Even the duffer deserves dignity. The reasonable responses to an offer of musical hospitality from a stranger are consent, an expression that the invitation is appreciated, cannot be accepted for the designated evening but might be on another occasion or a tactful expression of unwillingness. Occasionally, a response of the third kind is accompanied by an explicit analysis of the reasons that the one invited is too good to waste his time. This is gratuitous — one would not want a churl at his home, anyhow.

Equal Opportunity

A string quartet is an egalitarian organization. All that is needed is four players; race, creed, sex, nationality, age and previous condition of servitude are irrelevant. Whether or not prospective players have transportation is a consideration which militates against extremes in age, however. It is unlikely that a nonresident child will be leading your quartet. Often, an amateur quartet is assembled as a one-time group to share in the experience of trying to make music. If the experience is satisfactory, the same group may repeat it on another evening. Any player who does not enjoy the evening has the option of refusing to accept subsequent invitations, while it is the host's prerogative to decide who will be invited. Whether the quartet survives for a period of time as an entity with the same players depends on the civility — or, sometimes, on the tolerance of incivility — of its constituent players. The players need have nothing in common but their interest in making music, but friendships — and, alas, antagonisms — may develop among them. A less skilled player may receive more invitations than a good one if the others feel more comfortable with him. Later we will provide exposition on the sociopathology of amateur chamber music players.

A premise of this discussion has been that it is necessary to arrange a quartet session for an evening. This is based on the writer's experience, where weekday evenings were the only available times. Of course, there are large numbers of people for whom other times are more convenient. People who are homemakers with growing children might find it more convenient to find others with the same responsibilities who could arrange to play in the daytime. Some people who are retired are heavily recruited by other amateurs for daytime sessions. Chamber music is good any time of day or night.

Because a string quartet requires two violins, one violist and one cellist, a prospective arranger of a quartet evening needs to recruit three of these, unless, of course, the host has a family member who plays at the same level. There are a few amateurs who play violin, viola and cello with roughly equivalent facility, and there are many more who play both violin and viola. If only one violinist can be obtained, a satisfying evening can be passed playing string trios. If the violist or the cellist is the missing member, the evening can be salvaged if the defection is eleventh hour but it is better postponed.

Violinists should be motivated and encouraged to learn to play viola. The viola is easy to learn for a violinist, who can quickly attain the same level of competence — or incompetence — on both instruments. (Peace be to those professional violists who rail against violinists who consider the viola a "big violin" and do not give it the respect due its unique characteristics. This treatise is intended for those whose intentions cannot be realized by their executive ability.) Obviously, a player trying to arrange a string quartet session has more options if he or she can handle any of the three higher instrumental parts than in being locked in to one of the parts.

In the beginning, at least, one cannot afford to be very selective about the society microcosm constituted in an amateur quartet. Every new player one encounters contributes something, even if it is only a good anecdote. An evening that goes well, where the companionship was pleasant and the music produced approximated what it should sound like, can leave the player too euphoric to sleep. The evenings of frustration are banished from the memory, and the player looks forward to playing again. One daydreams of being wealthy and able to rent competent players or being influential, like a Supreme Court justice, able to commandeer competent and deferential players for a weekly quartet session, but this is but a dream. One settles for a quartet with three — no four — people whose technique does not match their ambitions.

II. The Home Salon

Physical Arrangements

The comfort of the players is the responsibility of the host. The host needs to provide four chairs—without arms—sturdy enough to withstand the body language and heft of the players and an area cleared of obstructions and extraneous noise. If this last requires a purchase of a color television set for an upstairs bedroom to keep good will between family members and musicians, the expenditure is small in relationship to the benefit. Potential disturbances to the players' concentration should be minimized. There should be room for instrument cases in the playing room and space cleared for coats in the guest closet.

Good lighting is essential. A strong light source overhead to provide even illumination on all the stands is helpful. A floor lamp in the midst of the players works well provided it does not obstruct communication among the players or provide glare. Lights affixed to the stands are another good expedient. Players over 40 tend to have diminished visual accommodation, so that their range for reading music is limited. Strong lighting helps. Players invited for the first time should be told if they need to bring along music stands. (The writer purchased secondhand metal orchestra stands from a local school, spray-painted them flat black to obliterate the graffiti and fixed portrait lamps with 40 watt tubular bulbs to them; a very satisfactory arrangement. The stands are suspended along cellar ceiling joists by hooks when not in use.)

The chamber used for the music session should be maintained at a comfortable and even temperature and humidity, conditions readily attainable with central heating and air-conditioning. Fans and room air-conditioners provide an uncomfortable level of exogenous noise to the group, and continual changes in temperature and humidity are certain to affect the pitch of the instrument strings. On a cold autumn evening in a den with a door leading to the garden, where the daughter of a quartet session hostess continually opened the door during the evening, there was inevitable deterioration of the endogenous noise produced by the group. Another quartet had just settled down to play during a rain storm when the cellist complained that a leak in the ceiling was directing drops of water on her head. She expressed gratitude they had not fallen on her cello, but she was volubly annoyed by the indignity to her person. The host procured a plastic container to catch the drops. With a unanimity not remarkable in their ensemble, the other players agreed that there would be a significant advantage for her playing—if not her posture—in moving the stands instead of asking her to balance the bucket on her head, the easier alternative.

There are few people who can set up rooms primarily for music; generally the most suitable space available is commandeered as an ad hoc chamber for the group. Nevertheless, there are some enthusiasts who have planned remodeling projects to provide for their music at home, building in lighting and music storage facilities. The guest player who does not acknowledge this effort and comment favorably is likely to be placed far down the invitation list for the next session.

Playing Al Fresco

Occasionally, we see television programs showing an out-of-doors chamber music session. It looks like a fine idea. Given enough distance from the neighbors, a string quartet is unlikely to receive a summons for noise pollution. There should be no problem with light for the players, and the fresh air and verdant surroundings should be beneficial to health and spirit. This is what an engineer friend calls a "good, unworkable idea." If the air is still, the insects are attracted by the players—even if the neighbors are repelled. Air is rarely still, however, and breezes turn pages before the players are through trying to read them. This leads to the adoption of devices to hold the music on the stands, such as magnets and lucite clothespins. These must be removed and replaced by the players, usually at different times. The profanity and/or scatological observations accompanying this operation are not consonant with enjoyment of playing. Another problem is temperature and humidity. The atmospheric conditions may be comfortable for the players, but instruments of the violin family voice displeasure at changes in environmental conditions. A fiddle kept in its case in a home with a controlled environment, air-conditioning in warm weather and heat and humidification when it is cold outdoors, may stay in tune for weeks. Even encased on a short trip to a music session, it often must be retuned.

Seating Arrangements

The arrangement of stands is a matter of judgment and preference, sometimes influenced by idiosyncratic hearing. Precedents can be found for any seating arrangement. Photographs of the Joachim and Kneisel quartets from about 1900 show the first violin seated facing the second with the cellist at the first's left; the Flonzaley used the seating adopted by American and most European quartets for performance, where first violin is stage front at audience left, second violin to his left, cello next to second violin and viola stage front to audience right. Some players take this arrangement as the one true string quartet seating plan. They react to a suggestion of a different relationship as they would to a heretic attacking an article of faith. (The writer prefers the usual British arrangement, with the viola between second violin and cello.) Because the home quartet is playing for its own enjoyment, not to an audience, performance practices are irrelevant. A mirror image to any of the seatings given above—or any other arrangement in the area—is workable so long as it is easy for the players to see each other without obstruction. Closest rapport is established by seating the quartet in a loose square.

The (Nonlending) Library

The impresario of the chamber music evening has responsibility for furnishing the music parts. If the host library is very limited, the guest players may be informed what it contains and invited to bring music along. Public libraries in large cities usually have collections of music for loan. One can also arrange to borrow music through ACMP. Serious amateurs, however, should set out to establish their own chamber music libraries over a period of time as their interests and finances dictate. Compared with other popular leisure activities such as tennis, jogging or philandering, amateur chamber music playing is much less expensive (as well as much less hazardous.)

Thus, the answer to a request from a player to borrow a quartet part for study at home should be, in substance, "I would love to make an exception for you, but it is our long-established policy that we never lend music to anyone." After that evening, the host may have no intention of inviting that player again unless desperate for a body, or the player may develop personal or business reasons for being unable to attend for some extended period of time. If this policy must be violated, the complete quartet should be lent, because ¾ of a quartet is unplayable. It will have to be replaced in its entirety if the part lent is not returned. Having one's own music library makes it possible to pencil in fingerings and remarks. It is considerate to have pencils easily available during chamber music sessions so that the guest players may make notes on your music parts — pencilled so that the notes may be erased or emended by subsequent users of the parts. A guest is well-advised to resist the temptation to inquire, "What damnfool idiot put in those stupid awkward fingerings?" Almost invariably, the "idiot" was his host.

Starting Time

Setting the starting time is a group decision. Once agreed on, the players should make every effort to be ready to play within 10 minutes of that time. Similarly, the length of time spent playing, who plays what part, and what music will be played all depend on mutual agreement. Much depends on the proclivities and physiology of the players. A typical evening chamber music session usually extends for three hours, with three to five works being played. The number of works played depends to an extent on their difficulty, familiarity to the players, their length and how many times repeats are taken or sections are repeated. Some quartet players insist on plowing straight through the music, with a minimum of repeats, as if they were being paid on a piecework basis. (These players often are equally insistent that all the repeats in the Minuet-Trio movement be played as written.) Others like to study one work in depth for one or more evenings. It is up to the quartet to reach a consensus. Instead of having someone shout "first ending" or "repeat" a measure before the decision is necessary, it is useful to adopt a convention beforehand, the recommended one being that the first repeat in a sonata-form movement is always honored and all the repeats in a theme and variations movement are taken. The second time through nearly invariably is better. Honoring repeats gives the players opportunity to make amends for errors on the first run-through — and commit different sins.

Recording

Recording equipment is available as an aid to study, but it is safer for the egos of any but a very advanced quartet to forego the opportunity to hear itself as others might hear it. Listening to recordings and attending performances of professional chamber groups is enjoyable and instructive. Comparing one's amateur efforts to these performances is naïve and demoralizing. A player may not realize for several measures that a key change has occurred, another may misread a leger note or may not recognize a flatted "F" as an "E." Major mistakes in rhythm, unlike intonation, usually cause a halt to gather forces. (It is often possible, however, to make compensating errors in timing within a measure or group of measures.) Better errors in execution should be allowed to vanish in the ether than be preserved within a magnetic matrix. Of course, errors in intonation and rhythm should not be accepted as the usual practice, but there should be a tacit understanding that some passages will require individual study in private.

Refreshments

Refreshments, such as tea and pastry, should be offered to the guests when the playing has finished for the evening. Some quartets offer wine and cheese at the conclusion of the evening, but these usually are groups that meet rarely. One might assume a rule that the less competent a player the host is the more elaborate the refreshments offered. There is no evidence in the writer's experience, however, to support this. A player may want to drink something between quartets, so light refreshment may be offered to all. Alcoholic drinks, with the possible exception of a single glass of beer or unfortified wine, vitiate the fine motor skills required of string instrument players — but the impairment of judgment may lead them to believe it helps. These should be deferred until the session is over — unless everyone partakes to even things out.

Auditors

The true amateur spirit demands that the players make music for its own sake and their own enjoyment. They are serious in their purpose, doing the best they are able even if the standard is D-level and trying always to do better. It requires a high level of cooperation to achieve a common purpose, and each player has a dependence on the others. The true domestic quartet does not need an audience; it is sufficient unto itself. Indeed, an auditor may detract from the give-and-take of the players and provide a distraction to them, interrupting their concentration on the music and the technical problems attendant with playing it. The chamber music lover who wants to hear it played "live" should attend a recital of professionals, thus hearing the music as it should be performed and supporting the art by paying for the privilege.

An incidental audience of one or more people may, nevertheless, be unavoidable — say a visiting relative or a spouse along to drive a guest player on icy roads. Of course, it should be understood that the auditors will be welcome to join in the refreshments after the instruments are stowed away for the evening, but the host should remind them — if necessary—they are not welcome as participants in discussions among the players or enfranchised as critics, even if they are moved by lack of musical sensibility or generosity to applaud. These strictures should be applied to nonplaying musicians—unless they have been engaged to coach the quartet. As one wag put it, "Amateur quartet playing is like any other human perversion. It should only be practiced by consenting adults in private."

III. By Any Other Name Would Smell...

Professionals

A professional string quartet needs a name with which to conduct their business. Names for these have been selected from countries, states, cities, schools, streets, instrument-makers, composers, painters, writers and players (usually the first violin.) Place names most often become misleading with time. The original Budapest String Quartet comprised Hungarians. The quartet by that name that achieved the reputation of the greatest of its time was composed of four Russian Jews naturalized in the United States. The problem with using a place name for a quartet is that society is mobile. A string quartet styling itself, "the Nineveh String Quartet" may have its key player move to Babylon. If they are professionals, the whole quartet moves to the new base of operations. Their sophisticated audiences realize that a place name tells of origins, not location.

Amateurs

Having a name for an amateur string quartet is pure conceit, unless it violates its pristine amateur status by performing for an audience. Nevertheless, many amateurs have adopted names for their quartets. One group, comprising four men of great girth and height, called themselves the Hafton String Quartet on the basis that their aggregate weight totaled a half ton. The name sounded vaguely musical, redolent of semi-tone. One may be surprised that no one has used the title, "The Ur String Quartet." This would allow the claim that the musicians play from "Ur-texts." The origin of "The Ill Tempered String Quartet" was explained in the Preface, and it is a continual source of fun. At its beginnings, when the players were too busy trying to maintain ensemble to bother about such niceties as the observance of dynamics, one player suggested "Semper Forte" as a title for the group. With time and effort, this became less appropriate. "Ill Tempered," however, has proved to be a sobriquet with staying power. Another amateur quartet, deciding to donate its services in a church fundraiser, styled itself "The Belmont," justifiably confident that none of those bidding for their services would question its credentials — at least until it was heard by the high bidder in the auction and his guests. A litigious audience might well have made a case for misrepresentation or at least consumer fraud in this instance.

IV. Staying in Shape

One year a friend, professional colleague and occasional quartet companion arranged a quartet session for us with a local scientist-player at a meeting held out of town. A year later, he telephoned and asked if I had heard about our host's lawnmower accident. He told me the unfortunate fellow had cut off the tips of the fingers on one hand. "Luckily," he added, "it was his right hand."

Henri Temianka told of a performance of the Paganini String Quartet, when the violist, Charles Foidart, dropped dead after finishing his solo in the Andante of the Haydn Op. 76, No. 3. The audience was surly about the abrupt ending of the concert. Up to the time their fiddling careers are terminated, usually less dramatically, many amateurs overcome physical disabilities to play. An acquaintance told of a home quartet evening where he was playing viola. "Suddenly," he said, "I had the sensation that the music pages were swimming around the room. I remember that the others grabbed first to rescue my instrument, then for me." He approved of these priorities, just as any fiddle player would.

It is not unusual for less serious infirmities to disappear during a quartet session. One player was so stricken with sciatica that he painfully lowered himself onto a chair at the beginning of the evening. As soon as the music making began, he felt fine, and he walked out briskly three hours later feeling no pain. Playing amateur string quartets does not guarantee physical fitness, but anyone who has spent three or four hours playing knows he has had physical exercise. Fiddlers tend to develop good upper body strength and firm handclasps. Walking, swimming and other good exercise can only help in building stamina for long quartet sessions. (Undoubtedly, good physical condition is beneficial in other activities, but the concern here is parochial.)

A Vl/Vla-A found in the ACMP Directory was found to be a feeble nonagenarian by the player delegated to take him to a session where he was to be first fiddle. He had to be assisted in walking, but he played with verve, vigor and perhaps a bit too much volume. Hearing loss is a concomitant of the aging process, and one that is difficult to overcome.

One should beware of committing exercise that may lead to injuries of the upper body, such as "tennis elbow." The first violin of the Guarneri learned to play tennis left-handed to protect his bow arm. It is noteworthy that a discipline has developed in medical practice devoted to the ills of professional musicians, who put unnatural stress on their bodies in their activities. Amateurs generally do not play often enough to suffer from these occupational hazards, although one frequent companion, retired from his profession, plays violin, viola and cello in quartets and orchestras nearly every day of the week as well as practicing for a weekly cello lesson. (With such versatility, he resolves his prospective host's logistics problems. He can play as often as he wants.) Injuries to the lower body, providing they enable one to sit, are tolerable. One may think of Itzhak Perlman, his legs useless as a result of childhood polio, who nevertheless maintains an outstanding career as a violin virtuoso and sometime chamber music player. What is considered so remarkable about him by many of us amateurs is that he keeps time perfectly without being able to tap his foot!

Practice Makes Passable

Practicing by oneself is worthwhile in keeping the physical equipment, bow arm and left hand, in good shape for the rigors of the quartet literature. If the player's technique is good, practice helps to maintain and extend it. If the player has bad habits, practice makes imperfect deplorable. Lessons are worthwhile if the player can afford the time and money. A good teacher can identify faults in technique and motivate practice — but why must teachers insist on assigning concertos, when duos and sonatas would be much more useful? Undirected practice can help facility in finding notes, but the player tends to ignore rhythm problems — unless he is tackling a particular problem or has a nature so unromantic that he can practice for an extended time with a metronome.

It is a sad fact that no matter how much one loves the music and how much romance there is in one's soul, expression of the love and feeling is limited by technique. Whether by taking lessons or analyzing technique problems and practicing seriously until they are resolved, the amateur has to attain a certain level of competence in order to find people who will play with him more than once. (It is better to try and fail than never to have tried. There are no "bad" players. Some of us just need experience. One might say that good playing comes from experience, and experience comes from recognizing errors.) We have a psychological defense mechanism which colors our perception of the sounds we produce. We sound better to ourselves than to our companions. One advanced amateur quartet arranged to present a recital at a church. They were well satisfied with their rehearsal, until the music director played a recording of it to them. The recital took place, but only after the quartet had hired a professional violinist to coach them. The pure amateur quartet gives no recitals, and their standards are such that they must satisfy only themselves.

One learns to play quartets by the playing of them, but the problems in finding the notes and playing them in time are much the same in other kinds of chamber music. Between quartet sessions, any opportunity should be seized to play duos and trios with other string instruments or a pianist. Some players maintain that orchestra rehearsals are useful in learning technique, and well they may be. One such skill is learning to turn pages rapidly with bow in hand, a valuable facility in playing chamber music.

Preparation

If there is a chance that the player may choose one of the quartets to be played at a scheduled quartet session, it is useful to read through all the parts beforehand and play at least one of them in the days before it. If a recording is available, it could be listened to with score in hand. (These laudable preparations are sometimes confounded when one arrives at the host's home to find an extra violist or cellist or learns that someone has defected and trios will be the repertory for the evening.) It may be useful to nap for 30–60 minutes after a light dinner before essaying a chamber music evening. If there has been no opportunity for practice in the days preceding, 15 minutes of scale practice may be useful in reminding the player to hold the instrument up, keep his left thumb from squeezing the fingerboard, use the whole length of the bow instead of only the six inches nearest its tip, grip the bow near the frog and exercise all of the other elements of good fiddling technique that should have been inculcated in his youth — but were not.

V. Of Bellies and Bows

The names used for the principal parts of our string quartet instruments in English, at least, might best be described as anthropomorphic — or gynecomorphic. The belly, back, head, neck, ribs and waist are derived directly from parts of the body. Almost miraculously, the evolution of function in the violin family led to the most beautiful of forms among the musical instruments. The curves of harps and guitars are attractive, but no instrument approaches the physical beauty of the violin family in form and finish.

The sound of the violin family depends on the dimensions, composition and curvature of the belly or top, the cut of the f-holes, the ribs or sides, the back, the bassbar, the soundpost, and the bridge and strings. The character of the sound depends on the vibrations set in motion by the rosined horsehair of the flexible bow held in the right hand and their interaction with the fingertip vibrations of the left hand on the strings. The scroll, pegbox, tuning pegs, fingerboard, tailpiece and end button are essential accessories. The instruments are complex; bellies being carved from one or more pieces of pine or spruce and backs, ribs, necks, fingerboards, peg boxes and scrolls from maple. Fingerboards are made from solid ebony, and tuning pegs, tailpieces and end buttons are of ebony, boxwood or rosewood. The belly wood is usually less impressive in grain than the back and sides, but it is embellished by the curves of the f-holes and the contrasting woods of the accessory parts. The colors of the varnished woods vary from yellow through amber to soft reddish hues and shades of brown. The striations and curls of the wood show through the transparent varnish with the play of light on the instrument. The effect of age and use of the instruments generally is one of added character from the shadings of colors caused by uneven wear on the varnish and, sometimes, the vestiges of repairs made over the decades. Bows, too, have beauty of form derived from function and ornamentation, but most of our aesthetic sensitivity is directed to the instruments.

Taking to the Lore

There is an immense body of literature and lore on all aspects of the violin family of instruments; their history, construction, makers, dealers and players, and — especially — those factors which affect tone. This is nearly matched by the literature on bows, the modern types dating from Francois Tourte (1747–1835) of Paris. Some bows, which were once "throw-ins" in outfits with the instrument and case, have become more expensive than many instruments as their playing characteristics and value as art objects has become recognized.

The violin as we know it was developed in the 16th century. The great Cremona makers began with Andrea Amati (*ca.*1520–1611) and culminated with Antonio Stradivari (1644–1737) and Giuseppe "del Gesù" Guarneri (1687–1745). The Amati family included Antonio (1550–1638) and Girolamo or Hironimus (1551–1635), Nicolà (1596–1684) and Girolamo (1649–1740). Reputedly, Nicolà was the teacher of Stradivari and Andrea Guarneri (*ca.*1626–1698). The Guarneri included Andrea's sons, Pietro (1655–?) and Giuseppe (1666–*ca.*1739), and his nephew, "Giuseppe del Gesù," so-called because of the IHS and cross on his labels.

Stradivari had two sons who worked with him. The instruments of Antonio Stradivari and Guarneri del Gesù are the most highly valued. Excellent violins, violas and cellos have been made in Italy, France, Germany, Great Britain, other European countries, the United States, Canada and elsewhere. (It is interesting that fiddles, like people, have nationality. The violin literature never fails to identify an instrument as Italian, German, English, French, and so on, even when the actual maker has not been ascertained.) Cottage industries and fiddle factories developed in Mirecourt in the Vosges region of France, at Mittenwald in Bavaria, at Bubenreuth in Germany and other centers for the mass production of instruments of the violin family.

Although these centers of violin-making housed artists who made fine instruments using their own labels, the bulk of their production was commercial instruments which could be made and sold cheaply. For many years, the mass production centers featured copies of the instruments of famous makers, complete with facsimiles of their labels. Some of these were finished to simulate the shading and wear patterns that come with age. The violin in grandfather's closet, labeled "Antonius Stradivarius Cremonensis faciebat 1721," may or may not include the words "Copy of" and "Made in Germany" or "Czechoslavakia," depending on its age. Many a discoverer of the family treasure has enjoyed a brief thrill of believing himself in possession of a priceless treasure until disabused of the notion on trying to cash in the fiddle for the fortune.

Most of these instruments look to the untrained eye like the real thing, but there is no way anyone can get satisfactory tone and response from most of them. Because they are cheap, it is the "Bohemian Strads" that are usually used as "student instruments." They provide a powerful deterrent to continuing study. Students may be able to learn the mechanics of playing on such execrable fiddles, but it is impossible for them to get satisfaction from an instrument without tonal response and nuance. Amateur chamber music players do not play Bohemian Strads for very long if they can afford better instruments. The frustration in trying to match the tone quality of their companions usually leads to an investment in a better instrument. The ear may fool the solitary player, but the quartet player has comparisons of his tone with three other instruments. He knows intuitively that the fault must be external to his technique and musicianship; it must be with his equipment.

What Price the Glory of Cremona?

The cost of a violin, viola, or cello is determined by a number of factors. These include the maker, country of origin, age, condition, tone, appearance and what the buyer is willing to pay. The famous-maker 17th and 18th century instruments are out of the price range of most of us amateurs, but it is possible to get instruments that sound good and are handsome at affordable cost. Instruments of the violin family are believed to improve with age; however, this can only be true of instruments that were well-made when new. Many a family closet yields an old instrument which proves to be a querulous-sounding product of some 19th century factory. As cheap wine does not age to perfection in the bottle, factory fiddles do not improve in closets. A hand-made modern instrument made in Germany may bring less money than an equivalent one made in Cremona, especially, or anywhere in Italy.

Appearance should be a less vital criterion than tone to the player; however, there can be no argument that a large part of one's satisfaction in using a violin, viola or cello derives from the esthetic component. An instrument with beautiful grain and attractive color will be prized more than one with equivalent tone, a plain-wood back and a dull finish. Bowed stringed instruments have value as art objects. In spite of advances in materials science and technology, regardless of countless studies directed toward their improvement, no one has advanced the art of construction of the violin family of instruments beyond that achieved by the Amatis, Stradivari and Guarneris more than 250 years ago. Apart from relatively minor changes in the early 19th century (lengthening the fingerboard, changing its angle and enlarging the bass bar), the form of violins, violas and cellos* has remained practically the same for centuries.

Violins are usually about 355mm (14 inches) in back length. Contrary to the dogmatic statement of one instrument seller we encountered, they vary by 2 to 3mm from this norm even in the works of the masters. The size of violas, which range from a back length of 375mm (about 14¾ inches) to more than 425mm (about 16¾ inches), and whether they have a head like that of a violin or like a cello, are sometimes the subjects of extended discussion at quartet sessions.

There are a few amateurs, notably American physicians, who can

---

*The discerning reader will have noticed that "cello" is used throughout this work, instead of the more pedantic "violoncello" or "'cello." Because "violoncello" derives from the Italian for small violone — and no one seems certain what a regular-size violone was — we will leave the word for the pedants who — with sounder rationale — call a "piano" a "pianoforte." The viola is often called the "Bratsche" in German scores, this being the Teutonic homonym for the Italian "braccia" from "viola di braccia" or arm viol.

afford authentic 17th and 18th century Italian instruments. (An amateur who played quartets at a summer music week with a physician who owned a genuine Stradivarius reported, "It was a pity the instrument could not play itself.") Beyond the esthetic component of enjoying a violin, viola or cello is its usefulness in impressing new quartet companions. A new player in a quartet may be depended on to give the others information on the history and provenance of his instrument, even if it has no distinguished label or even no maker's label at all. "Oneupsmanship" by the possessor of an authentic old Italian instrument vies with stories of the heirloom instrument that grandfather played or the product of a modern maker sure to become recognized as the peer of the old Cremonese geniuses in future generations. Some players will arrive carrying two fiddles, one to play and both to show and tell about.

Many of us subscribe to magazines and buy books that feature color photographs of instruments and bows made by famous artists. We study these carefully, trying vainly to understand the subtle differences in the shape of the scrolls and f-holes of the instruments and the camber of the bows described by the expert in the accompanying text. We marvel that the expert luthiers can identify the maker of an instrument or bow and fix the period in which it was made from subtle details of construction and varnish. Most of us are limited in expertise to distinguishing an amber-colored instrument from one that is red or yellow and identifying a one-piece back. Many of the violin dealers and repairers with whom we have personal contact are not among the cognoscenti, but few of them admit it. Looking at our own instruments and those of our companions, we take pleasure in the shading of the varnish, the voluptuous shapes of the body and scroll, the grain patterns or "flame" of the maple parts and the distinctive patterns that age and use — or abuse — produce on our instruments.

An excellent player will be an excellent player on a poor fiddle, but he cannot get out tone that is not built in. An unskillful player gains no facility merely by using a wonderful instrument, but the ability to produce good tone is an incentive for improvement. Most of us get the best instruments we can afford, given other priorities. Like the tennis player looking for the racket that will compensate for his slow reflexes and poor technique, most of us amateur quartet players are willing to suspend disbelief that a more expensive instrument or a new bow will minimize our technical problems. Indeed, many of us have been surprised by the improvement a better bow has made in our technique. (We begin by thinking of the bow as a mere accessory, like a chin-rest.) Go to an instrument dealer to get a bow rehaired or buy replacement strings, and the belief that better outfits help playing will be supported by the expert at the shop. "Someone who plays like you deserves a better fiddle, and, of course, a good fiddle demands a great bow and requires a fine case." Quartet players provide a good market for innovations in strings, chin and shoulder rests and other accessories which might, somehow, improve their sound and their technique. After all affordable innovations in equipment have been tried, we have no recourse to improve our playing but lonely and disciplined practice.

VI. Playing Second Fiddle

Origins of the Second Violin

In the middle of the 18th century, composers of music discovered that the combination of music for two violins, a viola and a cello provided them scope for their musical ideas. Music publishers found that there was a good market of amateurs willing to buy it. The string quartet has been the preëminent means of expression for composers of chamber music from that time to ours. The literature of string quartets is larger than that of string trios, quintets, sextets, etc. combined, and it is only approached in numbers by piano trios, another form that became popular among amateurs in the 18th century. Thus was born the social problem of the amateur string quartet, the second violin.

The Shame of It

Everyone who writes about string quartets deals with the pejorative implications of playing the second violin part. Playing second fiddle has become a metaphor, even among people who would not be able to distinguish a violin from a banjo, for anyone thrust in a secondary or subservient role. This connotation is a plague that afflicts both amateur and professional string quartets. The cellist is said to provide the vital bass line for the string quartet; the viola contributes its unique tone character to the group and its player "sits at the heart of the music." The first violin is the star, of course, distinguished further by the title used by the British, the "leader" of the quartet.

Alexander Schneider dropped out of the Budapest String Quartet for years, supposedly because he was bored with playing second fiddle.

The Guarneri String Quartet decided among themselves to give their second violin, John Dalley, first refusal on any music performances where only one violin was scored, such as a piano quartet or a string trio. The Emerson String Quartet violins, Eugene Drucker and Philip Setzer, alternate playing first and second in performances, either obviating the problem or sharing it. It is considered high praise for the second violin player in a professional quartet when the cognoscenti in the audiences worry during intermissions that he might defect to play first violin in another quartet.

Programs for string quartet performances discreetly list Messrs. Schlemiel and Schlemozl as "violins," but the audience knows who plays first, even if the group is not named the "Schlemiel — or Schlemozl — String Quartet." Publishers of quartet editions often designate the violin parts I and II. The generous intention is to indicate only that the violin parts are different. Similarly, Aulich and Heimeran suggested that the "first violin" and "second violin" designations be discarded in favor of "brother violins," but they did not consider the problem of which of the brothers was the elder who inherits the family title and fortune. No amount of sophistry will bleach the stigmata carried by the second fiddle. The discrimination is real. Even a veteran amateur quartet player like Joseph Wechsberg — who played first violin — wrote pityingly of the second fiddle "having to play endless pom-poms." On the other hand music historians point to Heinrich de Ahna, the original violist in the Joachim Quartet, who chose to play second violin when that player left.

The essence of chamber music is that each player has his own part. Compared to his counterpart in an orchestra, the quartet second fiddle has an exalted status indeed. Not only do all the second violins in an orchestra play the same part, but there is an institutionalized hierarchy among them based on how close they sit to the conductor compounded by their relation to the audience, the one further from it charged with turning pages. One quartet cellist, who squanders a potential chamber music evening by playing in an amateur orchestra, bemoaned the fact that the second fiddles had shown no improvement over several weeks of rehearsal and no evidence of practice at home.

It is a sad fact of the human condition that hardly any amateur practices second violin parts. Why this situation obtains has complex origins. Does the player subconsciously reject the label of "second fiddle" by ignoring the music until the time comes to play it? We offer this question as a potential thesis topic for a doctoral candidate in social psychology or semantics. Violists and bassists have banded together to advance the status of their instruments in solo recitals and concerti, but bassists are only occasional participants in chamber music, and string quartet violists have no ego problems. One might consider that an organization devoted to the advancement of the status of second fiddles might be useful, say a "Second Violin Anti-Defamation League." Such an association, however, would have few members. The only difference between first violin and second is the part; the instruments are identical, and the people playing them cannot be singled out of a crowd. Few violinists would proclaim their second fiddle status publicly.

A Digression

Let us at this point discuss the resources needed for amateur performance of works in the different genres. The string quartet is an ideally practical form. It requires a small number of players assembled at any mutually convenient time at home. Unlike a combination of wind instrument players, the volume of sound from a string quartet is unlikely to result in broken leases or complaints from the neighbors. An amateur orchestra requires a large number of string instrument players as well as a few woodwinds, brass and percussion players. This demands a conductor, a regular rehearsal time and the use of a suitable rehearsal hall. The conductor is usually a professional musican trying to get experience and recognition, which entails setting up three or four public concerts each year. The audiences for these concerts comprise relatives and friends of the players and, sometimes, a local music critic.

Amateur orchestras rarely perform Haydn symphonies, because they require small forces and clean playing. The conductors prefer to play romantic works which require large forces and diverse instrumentation, often bringing in "ringers" from professional ranks to take the front chairs for performances or fill special requirements in the score such as a bass clarinet or a harp. A good proportion of the conductors of amateur orchestras aspire to direct opera. They would much rather

be involved with opera than symphonies. After they begin feeling comfortable in their posts, they schedule performances of the Mahler works
with voice, then arrange for concert performances of operas.

The conductors serve at the pleasure of the orchestra members,
and one too many performances where the orchestra accompanies
singers — two or three in all — incurs the displeasure of its membership.
Conductors of amateur orchestras rarely have long tenure. Operas require an orchestra, scenery and singers. These are nearly impossible for
amateurs to manage, but they are sometimes approximated by
chamber performances with a pianist substituting for the orchestra or
a concert performance with the solo singers standing in front of the orchestra and a chorus massed in the rear. In many such concert performances, the performers outnumber the audience.

An amateur orchestra serves as recreation for its players and as a
stepping-stone to recognition for its conductor. Public performance is
an expression of its reason for being. The domestic string quartet, in
contrast, exists principally for its players. They need no audience for
fulfillment of their objective, which is to make music for its own sake
and their own enjoyment.

Second Best?

Granting that the second fiddle in a string quartet may arrive at
this stand because his technique or experience is inferior to the first,
sometimes the roles depend more on personality than ability. The truth
of the matter is that playing second violin may require better musicianship, as distinct from technique, than playing first. One of the faculty
at a summer chamber music session for amateurs remarked that most
of the players are not avid for instruction; she avers her principal function is to play second violin in their quartet sessions. One might think
that the amateurs would insist that the professional violinist should
play the first violin part, thus achieving the best musical results. Apparently, this advantage is offset by eliminating the problem of which
paying player is relegated to second fiddle. Moreover, an exceptional
second violin player is the glue that holds together the ensemble. It is

37

arguable that the solution arrived at for social reasons is not the better.

Who plays second violin in an amateur string quartet is a social problem if the ability of the violinists is close in the subjective opinion of either. (It has been noted that each player hears a distortion of the music he produces, confounding the knowledge of what is actually produced with what is intended, while every mistake in rhythm, intonation or dynamics of the violinist at the neighboring stand is accurately recorded.) Where one violinist is an excellent player and the other only fair, it is usually considered a waste of resources to tolerate the less skilled one as first fiddle for more than an occasional excursion. Nevertheless, the lesser violinist should be given opportunity to play first for one quartet in an evening. The fiddler so appeased realizes he is being "thrown a bone," but he is grateful nonetheless. There exists a tiny minority of violinists who will play only the second violin part, motivated either by nobility or timidity. There are violinists who can only play first violin, giving poor accounts of themselves if assigned to the second's chair. Although the violin playing aspects of the first's part may be more difficult than the second fiddle's, the fact that the first leads makes his part of the ensemble easier.

The music for the second violin rarely rises past the third position on the E-string in quartets of Haydn, Mozart and early Beethoven, while the first violin may soar in the highest reaches of the instrument. The professional string quartet began when Beethoven's aristocratic friends subsidized a quartet led by Schuppanzigh, which served as a laboratory for the composer. Since that time, early in the 19th century, the second fiddle has had technical challenges and his share of voice-leading. Only occasionally does the second violin have a melody to play for any extended length of time in music of the classical period; these are the province of the first fiddle. More often, the second fiddle plays in harmony with the first or the lower "voices" of the quartet, or he plays a rhythmic or accompaniment line.

Composers wrote for the resources available to them and to accommodate the demands of their patrons and public. For example, Haydn wrote 126 trios for baryton, a now-obsolete viol played by his employer, Prince Nicholas Esterházy. Haydn's staff of musicians always included one excellent violinist, so that he was able to write virtuosic first violin parts in his quartets with confidence they could be played well. Nevertheless, Haydn and other composers wrote for four parts, all of which were indispensable to the whole. Where the second violin — or another of the parts — is playing "endless pom-poms" or other repetitive figures, it is a part conceived by the composer as necessary to the collective effect of the four voices.

It requires a sense akin to craftmanship for the second violin to listen to the others and fit in his contribution accurately and with proper style. Doing this well gets recognition from one's companions but, best of all, a sense of achievement as a musician. Occasionally in classical quartets, the second violin is called on to lead with a melodic line or change tempo. A notable example is the extended solo in B♭ minor for second violin in two variations of the slow movement of Haydn's Op. 74, No. 2. A second fiddle hesitant to seize his opportunities is unfortunate.

The second fiddle sometimes is the weak link in a quartet of amateurs, but the music demands he be an equal. The second violin, being familiar with the first's part, can provide support in "black note passages," where the natural tendency of the first, with 32nd and 64th note passages in front of him, is to compound the difficulty by speeding up; an error endemic in amateur string quartet-playing. A second who takes pride in ensemble will cover mistakes by the first by conforming to small errors in rhythm when necessary instead of keeping a metronomic pulse, pointing these out, sometimes tactfully, at an appropriate stopping point. A mischievous second, on the other hand, can subtly increase the tempo before the thicket of notes for the first is reached. Playing second violin well is an art close to the heart of chamber music. A violinist who cannot play second violin is not a true quartet player. One friend scorns such people, who must always be allowed to play first violin, as "soloists." Temianka, however, tells of famous violin virtuosi, invited for an evening of chamber music at his home, trying to beat the others to the second violin desk.

Take the First Second

An attorney who played violin, scouting a retirement home in Florida, asked at one development if anyone there played string quartets. Within an hour he was led to a home where chairs and music stands were arranged in a square, and the first violin part of a Haydn volume was placed on the stand in front of him. Moments later, the other players arrived. The other violinist looked at the second violin part at the unoccupied stand, wordlessly exchanged it for the first violin part, then declared in tones that brooked no argument, "That's my part!" Being first violin may be a privilege won by superiority in technical ability at playing fiddle; it is as often simply one that is arrogated by force of personality.

The first violin in a quartet is first among equals. Although the others have the right — and exercise it — to dispute his choice of music, tempo, dynamics and interpretation, the first fiddle leads the consensus. If the first is indisputably the best player present among the violinists (the violist may be one, too), a Vl-A playing with -C's, this is established when the first page of the quartet has been played. Let the first be merely equivalent or only marginally superior to the other fiddle players and a potential for discord exists. The first violin must have an underdeveloped sense of shame and the "chutzpah" of a pickpocket at a police convention, being willing to take his chances on correctly identifying a note high above the staff in an unfamiliar quartet and work through a fast passage with tricky changes in rhythm. If the odds are even he can get it right, this constitutes an acceptable challenge. If the first violin apologizes to the others for his errors in execution after fouling a rhythm or fluffing a passage high on the fingerboard, he risks losing credibility and authority. The second violin and, often, the violist know in their souls that *they* could have played those passages flawlessly, with verve and musicality.

The true first violin personality never explains, never excuses. If the first violin commits an egregious error, he magnanimously shares responsibility for the break in the flow of the music, perhaps mumbling something like, "We weren't together at letter 'F,' let's take it again at the double bar." Just because he admits to being a paranoid personality does not mean that the "second" and the viola are not out to get him. He notices and bitterly resents that the second is fighting him on tempo and trying to lead, and the viola and cello play too loud. The effective first quells any revolts ruthlessly; the music demands it must be so. Even if the first violin changes roles with others during the evening, playing second fiddle or viola in other quartets, while he has the responsibility of playing first violin, he must either exercise control or lose it. The first fiddle who can only carry off those quartets he has studied is an imposter who will be unmasked by his fellows when an unfamiliar quartet is selected.

The "Big Fiddle"

Viola players, during the 18th and much of the 19th centuries, mostly were recruited from the refuse of violinists—and the ranks of toothless horn players—according to the composers Berlioz and Wagner. During the 18th century, the violas available were of large size, too cumbersome to play in high positions, so that the music written for the instrument was technically undemanding. The mature Mozart, who enjoyed playing the instrument, wrote some gratifying parts for violists, however. Since there is but one violist in a string quartet, this player does not bear the sociological stigma of the second violin. The viola has a tone distinctive from that of the violins and cello, and it shares responsibilities—and opportunities for mischief—with the other middle voice, the second fiddle. Chamber music from the 19th and 20th centuries provides some glorious solo passages for viola and many technical challenges. If the violinists cannot play viola, the violist can demand the deference normally accorded the cellist, for the string quartet cannot function without him, and the quality and quantity of the literature for string trios with viola are better than those without.

Most violists began as violinists and many play both instruments as the occasion demands, but there is an increasing number of young players who were trained on viola from the beginning and who do not play violin. These are generally selected by school music teachers on the basis of their height. The gangly youths are judged better equipped to handle the larger instruments than their smaller classmates. Just as a clarinet player can learn saxophone easily and the reverse does not hold, a violinist can learn viola quickly, but someone trained from the beginning as a violist has great difficulty taking up violin. The beginner is better served by starting on violin and switching later.

A violinist learning to play the viola has one major problem, the viola clef. Some violinists start out playing the viola only in the first position while reading as if they were in third position on the treble clef, but it is more useful to learn how the clef determines fingering on the viola. I found it useful to buy a transcription of the Bach cello suites for viola. After I could play through the first two reasonably well, within a week, I could read viola music nearly infallibly in quartet sessions. It took longer to be able to switch from viola to the violin during a quartet evening without starting a major third off.

Prince of Players, the Cellist

There are few violinists and violists who play quartets who would not wish to be reincarnated as cellists. The cellist has nearly as eminent a role in the string quartet as the first violinist, with a large share of beautiful melodies and without the responsibility for leading. Many of those violinists and violists who learn to play cello well in their present incarnation abandon the higher-voiced instruments. Although learning to play the viola acceptably is very easily accomplished without formal instruction for someone who plays the violin, involving an automatic adjustment to the difference in size of the instrument and adapting to reading the viola clef, learning to play the cello requires a new technique.

A string quartet has a measure of redundancy in its complement of two violins and a viola, especially if the violinists can play viola. The cellist, on the other hand, is irreplaceable. Without a cellist, the others have meager musical fare. Certainly, a quartet is impossible without a cellist. Should the cellist fumble a cantilena in the thumb position or do a *portamento* through a series of sixteenth notes marked *staccato*, it is remarked on only by the violist if at all. The cellist is treated with deference; no one comments if he shows up after everyone else has tuned save to indicate gratitude at his safe arrival. He is provided the most comfortable chair, the others laugh at his witticisms whether or not they understand them or have heard them many times before, and he is offered first choice of dessert. It may appear to the casual observer that the first violin is the important personage in a string quartet, but the cellist knows better. Cellists have well-adjusted psyches, unlike the sometimes manic first and depressive second fiddles. Cellos cost more than violins and violas of equal merit to purchase, maintain and transport, but parents of small children with musical talent can balance the additional cost against the assurance of mental health and sweet personality that comes with playing cello when deciding on an instrument for their boy or girl.

Versatility

There is an advantage to being able to read through all four parts of a quartet in practice, and there is a great satisfaction in being able to play at least three of the parts. (Second violinists, if they practice at all between chamber music sessions, hardly ever practice their own parts; they play through the first violin music.) A practical advantage in playing violin and viola is that it increases one's opportunity to play, but, further, there is intellectual stimulation in playing one part of a quartet with experience in having played one or two of the others. In a quartet where three of the players are able to handle the violin and viola parts (which has not been infrequent in the later years of the Ill Tempered String Quartet), it is enjoyable for each of them to play all three parts during a quartet evening, and the experience is valuable for future readings of the music played. Quartets where this practice is common do not suffer from the second violin syndrome.

Another advantage of being able to play both violin and viola becomes apparent when the violist is late (defined as 10 minutes beyond the agreed on arrival time) or cannot keep the commitment. There is enough good literature for violin, viola and cello to play until the violist arrives or for an entire evening if necessary—providing one of the violinists can switch to viola. Literature for two violins and cello, on the other hand, is both less available and less interesting. (Much of this derives from the baroque era of trio sonatas, a form for keyboard instrument, two treble instruments and bass. The keyboard usually employed was the harpsichord, which affords no change in dynamics and a weak bass line. Thus, the cello repeated and strengthened the bass line of the harpsichord. Treble instruments could be two violins, violin and flute, or oboe and violin. Although much baroque music is very beautiful, one often is reminded of Harold Schonberg's epigram that it "repeats itself in regular patterns, like wallpaper.") This versatility is useful, too, when a fifth player is invited, affording the means for a two-viola quintet. (The second viola or second cello in a string quintet, being a relatively infrequent role, appears to suffer no "second fiddle" discrimination.)

It is obvious that all components of a string quartet are essential; that the second fiddle stigma is a silly prejudice. Nevertheless, it exists, and second violin players in amateur quartets are affected by it. The most effective solution is to allow the violins to change roles occasionally. If one or both of the violins can play viola and the violist is also a violinist, these parts can be interchanged. All of the players will be better musicians for the experience.

VII. The Sociopathology of the String Quartet

Amateur string quartet players are often people of considerable attainment in their vocations, people who evince charm in their intercourse with others in their professions or in ordinary social situations. That this civilization is a veneer may become apparent in the high stress situation existing in an amateur string quartet. Whatever their social status may be outside the realm of amateur music becomes irrelevant. They lay their egos bare in coping with the music. Trying to play above one's level of competence in a quartet provides a cruel test of character. We concentrate all our physical and mental abilities on the music, and anything which assaults this concentration is resented on an elemental, sometimes childish, level. It may be helpful to provide a catalog of some of the types encountered in an amateur string quartet with continually changing complements of players.

Amateur string quartets that meet regularly with the same players may endure for years, some coming together at predetermined times, like a team in a bowling league. No doubt this arrangement serves the music much better than the quartet arranged the previous weekend for a midweek evening with whoever can come. Yet, there is a sense of adventure in arriving at someone's doorway, double case for violin and viola in hand, not knowing who two of the players are, what will be played and which instrument will be required. This casual quartet allows for a great range of experiences in string quartet playing — sometimes pleasant, sometimes painful, always interesting.

A stranger invited to join three people who have played together is no longer an outsider by the time the first quartet has been played. By the time the instruments are packed away, a relationship has been established—for better or worse. Sometimes, it continues in other sessions. Whether or not it works depends only partially on instrumental proficiency; personality is a large factor. An amateur quartet is a voluntary association. Joachim called his string quartet a four-voiced democracy, and this may be true with respect to interpretation of the music. In the amateur "catch-as-catch-can, no holds barred" quartet, those who serve as the hosts decide who will be enfranchised as citizens of this democracy.

Distinguished Antecedents

Almost invariably, the player with a European accent, invited to play for the first time, will casually mention his training at "The Conservatory," daunting the others with visions of some formidable equivalent of the Juilliard School or Indiana University School of Music. After playing has proceeded a short time, the others may discern that "conservatory" must be one of those words that is a false cognate, probably meaning whatever place the local fiddle teacher in the homeland of that guest gave lessons to the children of the local burghers. There is no way to check on the claim if one wanted to do so. That town was devastated in The War. Another may claim to be a student of a distinguished professional instrumentalist. Alas, that virtuoso performs now for the Angels.

Tools of the Trade

All of us try to get the best instruments we can afford, granting that price is not necessarily directly related to sound. Given that the financial priorities of our companions are not known to us, it is bad form to criticize the tones emitted by the other players. Often there is legitimate doubt of whether the unpleasant sound produced by a companion is due to deficiencies in the instrument or its player. We nearly always blame the player, and we are usually correct. It sometimes happens that a player who expects to play only violin or viola for a session and has brought only one of his instruments will be asked to play the other. Then comes the necessity to play on another's instrument. The question is then resolved, for the player on the borrowed instrument feels he has eliminated ability as an alternative to consider.

Some players continually take their instruments to the shop for touch-ups of minor varnish defects, use expensive fittings such as box-wood tailpieces and pegs inlaid with ebony and keep their fiddles scrupulously clean. They keep their instruments in canvas-covered, plush-lined fitted cases that may cost more than their companions' instruments. Others ignore the beginnings of separation between belly and ribs as long as the buzzing it causes is not too noticeable, allow rosin to coat the strings and whiten the belly of the instrument and use tuners on all four strings like country music fiddlers. Cellists may appear with their instruments in worn canvas bags and violinists and violists with leatherette-covered cardboard cases patched with electrician's tape.

The fastidious instrumentalists look with scorn on their slovenly companions. It is more of the frustrations of some amateur players that the appearance of an instrument bears little relation to the ability of its player. A player considering purchase of a new instrument will sometimes bring two or three to a session to get the opinion of his companions, but perfect harmony in their opinions is as rare as it is in their ensemble. In the end, the decision on purchase of an instrument is as personal as the choice of a person to marry. After the decision has been made, however, the consequences of a change in heart on the instrument are invariably less expensive.

Occupational Hazards

Wechsberg advised, "Never have a gynecologist in your quartet," telling the story of his first quartet experience, pressed into service as second fiddle when the obstetrician in his uncle's quartet was called away on the quartet evening. This is good counsel only when the OB-Gyn specialist is the cellist or the only violist. If one must have a physician in a quartet, choose a specialist in something like dermatology or radiology. One might extend this injunction to real estate agents, who may have to "close a deal" in the evening, and to mothers of small children. One young mother called an hour before quartet time to tell the host the baby-sitter had defaulted. The evening was salvaged when the host agreed she could bring along her two-year-old child. The tot was awed by the quartet, sat quietly and was soon asleep. Next time, the mother decided to save the cost of a baby-sitter; however, the child, now familiar with the group (and, perhaps, an incipient music lover), stayed awake and demanded to be taken home at frequent and inconvenient intervals. Other players were recruited for subsequent sessions.

Worshippers at the Altar of Music

Although all quartet players must be serious about their attempts to make music, the intentions of many amateurs, especially beginners, cannot be realized with the ability they have. They compensate for this by hearing more of what is intended than what is actual, much as one can enjoy a broadcast of fine music heard on a poor receiver. Let them be thrown into the company of a musical puritan for a casual evening, and the atmosphere becomes miasmic. The puritan may have started out playing badly years before, but he has achieved competence — not necessarily excellence — and he dismisses the painful memory of his beginnings. He professes a profound reverence for the great composers, and he considers it a desecration to play a great work badly. He feels an almost evangelical obligation to castigate the wicked for their sins in rhythm, intonation and dynamics. Thus unnerved, they play worse than before. Curiously, if invited a second time to play with these musical vandals, he agrees to come. Perhaps the reason for a second invitation and acceptance is similar to that offered for second marriages — the triumph of hope over experience.

Sadists and Masochists

One recruit as first violin boasted to the others at his first session of his experience at "whipping a piano trio into shape." It was unaccountable to him, he complained, that just when he had them playing up to his standard, the pianist and cellist dropped out of the group. He announced cheerfully that he intended to "whip this quartet into shape." The player who served as host decided it would ennoble his character and improve his understanding to continue to invite this fellow, while the other sometime host refused. This arrangement endured a few weeks until the first fiddle criticized his host's interpretation of an accompaniment figure. His name disappeared from the calling list. Perhaps, somewhere, this "first" has located some masochistic music makers.

It is acceptable to three players in a quartet if the fourth is critical of the way the quartet played—or misplayed—a passage or a movement, provided that the word "we" is not used. Each of the three players knows the criticism is valid for the other two, but he is tolerant and sees no gain in humiliating the offenders. Use of the first person plural, as in "We really murdered that piece," is an accusation of collective guilt. Each of the other players believes the misdeed was committed in spite of his heroic efforts to maintain ensemble. It is not good manners to single out a player as an offender. All amateur quartet players empathize with the spirit of the legendary sign in a western saloon, "Don't shoot the piano player. He's playing as good as he can." If the piano player owns the only saloon in town, the warning is especially valid. Nevertheless, the temptation is sometimes irresistible.

Audience Participation

Despite the principle that auditors have no place at an amateur quartet session, they must occasionally be tolerated. Sometimes they must be reminded, gently if possible, that they are welcome participants in conversations only during refreshment time when the playing is over. One evening, the husband of one of the players decided to sing along with the quartet. When the unnerved host stopped the quartet and objected, the singer's wife remarked, "Oh, he has such a beautiful baritone." "Sure he does," replied the host, "but the only string quartet I know of with an added voice part uses a mezzo soprano."

Beating Time

One might infer by watching that there are many amateur quartets written for strings and percussion. One of the players can be seen, heard and even felt stamping out the beat like a flamenco dancer. Where there is more than one of these, nearly invariably the beats differ slightly, leading still another player to yell "One" at the beginning of a measure in an attempt to restore synchrony. Sometimes this works, but it often destroys concentration and brings the music to a halt while the players vote on how many were actually at "one." Most times the vote ends inconclusively in a tie.

The experienced player will feel the pulse of the music in his brain and adjust to changes in rhythm from the clues given by his partners. The less rhythmically-secure player needs to do something to help him play in the right place at the right time. Some players find it useful to mouth the count silently. This looks terrible for an audience, but there should be no audience. If the foot banger is the first violin, a suggestion from one of the players that they would tolerate stocking feet may lead to a solution, if it is accepted, or at least a temporary inhibition of the vigor of the pounding. If the stamper is the second or the viola, problems are almost inevitable. He often follows the beat he generates instead of following the leading "voice." This may lead to a contest of wills with no winners.

It is useful for the first violin or whoever starts a section to count "one measure for nothing." If the first is a foot stamper, all goes well until he reaches some difficult passages, where he is faced with a difficult subconscious value judgment — play the notes in tune or in time. Sometimes he compromises, reaching for the right notes and stamping his foot in synchrony with the rhythm he adopts instead of the one he began with. If he does not exaggerate the liberties taken, good players can accommodate to him. (Sometimes the only workable arrangement in a quartet is to let the violinist with the weakest rhythm play first violin. The writer got much of his first violin experience this way.) One violinist, playing first in Haydn's Op. 77, No. 2, announced before beginning the slow movement that he had an extended passage in 64th notes and would slow up there. The violist looked at him pleasantly and stated, "Play the music! The notes are *your* problem, not ours."

Tuning

Let one player check tuning at some stopping point, and the compulsive tuner in the quartet joins in immediately with fortissimo fifths. Not infrequently, this same person is the "concerto player"; he has painfully worked out and memorized one passage from a bravura work and presents it at this time for the edification and admiration of his fellows. Often, it is the best he sounds all evening. Another player, secure in his tuning, uses the time to look ahead to the upcoming passages and practice the difficult parts—there are many. If the first player needs to adjust his tuning, he cannot hear above the cacophony.

Look, Ma, I'm Playing Quartets

It is not unusual that the novice quartet player is exhilarated by the realization that he is actually holding down his corner of the music. He conveys this thrill to his companions by singing out *forte* no matter what the dynamics notations are on the score. An ungentle reproof from one of the others or, worse, a python-scale "Sshh!" destroys his concentration, and he loses his place. He then plays *sotto voce* while he assembles clues to his whereabouts in the flow of the music. A resumption at a high decibel level is the signal that he has returned. The others must be tolerant and recognize that this proclivity will be outgrown with experience—likely within a year or two of regular playing.

Interpolations

The raconteur in the group is often reminded of a story too good to wait until the quartet is finished for the evening. This is a cause of great anguish to the "pieceworker," the player in the quartet who takes pride in the number of quartets that can be read through in one evening, resenting interruptions for stories, time taken for repair of mangled passages and decisions to observe marked repeats.

Xenophilia and -phobia

Quartet players occupy a spectrum between the repertory players and the adventurers. The first are those who learned the parts of three or four string quartets. They have to be shamed and coerced into playing music which is not familiar to them. The adventurers are players who are intent on expanding their experience by trying new music, often too difficult for them and their companions. Having adventurers promotes more bad temper displays in a quartet, but it may lead to improvement if the new challenges are conquered. This is not to say that the players cannot read a Haydn or Mozart that none of them has played before or for a long time, because they are familiar with the genre. The Franck quartet or a late Beethoven from the 19th century may be as new to the players as a quartet just published by a modern composer.

To maintain some semblance of civility, we recommend that the players adopt a rule that only one quartet new to the players can be tried during any one evening and that its proponent should have practiced it beforehand or — at least — have listened to it. Often, a quartet will be selected for trial on the basis that one of the players heard it presented by a famous ensemble at a recent concert or may have heard it broadcast on the drive to the session. There is usually no reluctance from the others to try it. At one such reading, the first violin, who had proposed playing a specific quartet, pontificated that the Guarneri String Quartet plays it thus, the Juilliard String Quartet plays it so, but he prefers playing it as the Guarneri does. "I would be happy if you could play more of the notes in tune without worrying about sounding like the Guarneri or the Juilliard," said the exasperated violist. Of course, he was never invited to play with that violinist again. He had "plugged the piano player." He knew when he made his comment that he would be shunned forevermore by the host; the trade-off was worthwhile.

Cognoscenti and Ignoramuses

The "musicologist" is the player who volunteers information on the background of the music being played, e.g., that it was composed on a Tuesday when the master had dyspepsia and revised later during one of his bouts of syphilitic paresis. This autodidact is an avid reader of books and journals on music as well as concert program notes and record liners. He may or may not play well. Some companions may find his information interesting; others are annoyed. With players who have fiddled together often enough that they have stopped trying to be polite to each other, the volunteer pedagogue may elicit a *viva voce* groan and a remark such as, "The Office of Unimportant Information has been heard from for this evening. Let us continue with the music." The true musicologist is undaunted and unrepentant. The antipode to the musicologist in the quartet is the invincible ignoramus. He knows Haydn quartets only by the number at the top of the first page. If asked to propose a quartet to play, he might call for Haydn number 13 or 72, and he neither knows nor cares that the first, Op. 77, No. 1, was written decades after the second, Op. 33, No. 3. If the invincible ignoramus is an excellent player, the musicologist grumbles at the injustice of this situation for days after.

Paragons of Virtue

Those noble souls who encourage their inferiors with praise for good efforts, overlook faults which cannot be remedied and provide tactful instruction for those which can are found rarely. Such paragons are sometimes the better-playing half of an unequal "mama and papa" team, having repressed the expression of feelings of impatience and intolerance towards their less skilled mates in years of working to keep their marriages intact. When a player responded to an observation from one such "mama" on his improvement from the year before with the statement, "I had only one direction to go—up," she inspired him further with, "Ah, but you could have stayed where you were."

Playing a string quartet requires sensitivity to the feelings of and reactions to the actions of other people. It is a cooperative venture, but there is no denying that often there is an element of competition. Playing well brings ego satisfaction; playing poorly—or inferring disapproval from the others—is ego-wounding. It is often stated that amateur chamber music playing is a very civilized recreation. The validity of this statement is thrown open to question by the activities of a quartet of not very competent players.

Amateurs vs. Professionals

A professional string quartet comprises players who have few if any technical problems in the music they play for a living. One may read about the year or more after formation that the quartet spends in preparation before their public debut and their meticulous rehearsals for the 20 or so works they will offer in a concert season. Helen Ruttencutter's book on the Guarneri String Quartet is instructive, mentioning in passing that the Flonzaley Quartet rehearsed for a year before their debut. The professionals work on achieving near perfection in their interpretation of the music, trying to achieve unanimity of ideas on tempo, dynamic balance and expressiveness. There is no question about who plays which part, the roles remaining constant for as many as 20 years or more. Certainly the players love the music, but they are playing for a living. The public and most critics demand near perfection in technique, individuality in interpretation and charisma in performance.

Nevertheless, the amateur can only be heartened in reading reviews such as this one on a London recital: "Without some ugliness, of tone or proportion, it's difficult to convey either the intellectual or technical arduousness of a piece like Beethoven's Op. 131 or its facetious side. The Endellion Quartet's unfailing beauty of sound and their impeccably tasteful phrasing here exceptionally worked against the music by narrowing its expressive range." Perhaps we amateurs are expressive in our occasional beauty of tone and catch-as-catch-can phrasing. It is difficult to believe the critic meant exactly what he wrote. Sometimes a critic will praise an ensemble with the words, "they play as one man (or one instrument)," a virtue sometimes realized by some professional string quartets and one not to the writer's taste. One enjoys listening to four different personalities in a quartet. If you want to hear someone playing as one man, listen to one man. We hear a virtuoso playing the Paganini caprices, the Bach sonatas and partitas for solo violin or the Bach suites for unaccompanied cello and wonder how one person can manage all those notes and make music from them.

VIII. Ripping the Rembrandt

The amateur string quartet is like the professionals only in that they may essay some of the same literature on similar instruments, just as a weekend tennis player is like a professional in that he plays with the same equipment by the same rules. There are amateurs that play almost to professional standard. This should be the ultimate goal of all amateurs—even if it may never be realized. It has been noted above that some amateur chamber music players are professional musicians, including teachers and orchestra players, who play quartets for pleasure. These may often play quartets nearly on a professional quartet level. Most amateurs, however, cannot hope to play that well. These do not have the neuromotor equipment of the professional that enables the latter to do easily what cannot be done without great difficulty, if at all, by amateurs. It is a distinction between genius and talent. One stands in awe of genius, but talent, too, must be respected. The ability to play a stringed instrument well enough to attempt to play chamber music is no mean accomplishment, even if the level of proficiency attained is not high. It requires innate ability to discriminate pitch and rhythm, talents which can be improved with training and experience. The amateur recognizes his own limitations—and those of his playing companions even better—and tries to transcend them. He does something else for a living, sometimes achieving distinction at it, but quartets are played for recreation.

Many amateur chamber music players are able to arrange regular quartet sessions with the same companions, these arrangements sometimes lasting for years. The Ill Tempered String Quartet, on the other hand, comprises the writer and any three other people. This group may be constant for weeks at a time, but it is frequently necessary to find one or more players at a given time. (If the writer should arrange two quartet sessions in a week with six different players, both quartets are called the ITSQ. This felicitous situation rarely obtains.) A quartet may be arranged for a weekday evening on the weekend previous, and only the third person invited and the host know who the other players may be. Thus, one or two of the players may arrive at the appointed time without knowing in advance whether they will be playing first, second or viola, if they play violin and viola, and without knowing what music will be attempted. Such an ad hoc quartet spends much time sight-reading. Of course, there is a difference in reading a familiar work and in trying something one has never played before. Sometimes the player is familiar with one of the parts and is called on to play another. Surprisingly, it is often more difficult for someone accustomed to playing a first violin part to play the second violin than the converse.

Selection of Quartets

The amateur quartet is sometimes advised to restrict itself to those quartets it can handle technically. Aulich and Heimeran, for example, proscribe late Beethoven quartets for the amateur, suggesting that mangling of these masterpieces is sacrilege. One could argue in rebuttal that this is no more a sacrilege than hacking Haydn or maiming Mozart. Most of the quartet literature available for purchase consists of masterpieces, often the finest work of the composer in any medium. The lesser works often are either out of print and available only in archives or inordinately expensive. It may seem prudent never to try to play works that are too difficult technically and musically. Yet, how can one determine his limitations without exceeding them?

There is a great elation attained in managing to play tolerably through a middle or late Beethoven or a Brahms quartet for the first time, after many failed attempts and strained friendships. That which is obscure and unplayable one year may be lucid and tractable a year or so later. As in any other field of knowledge a base is constructed slowly; at some point a miracle of cognition may occur and a revelation be created. It may never happen, but the process should be given a chance. The closer one approaches proficiency on technically difficult work, the better one does on work within one's grasp. (It might be observed that technical difficulty does not necessarily equate with musical superiority.) Let no one set boundaries. If the quartet members are willing to try to read through — or, better, study — a late Beethoven, say, in private, it is their own business. Muscles unstretched atrophy.

Limitations

There is a classic joke about a drunk who claims he knows his capacity for liquor — but he always passes out before he reaches it. The chamber music player continually tries to enlarge his capacity for the literature. It might be easier on him and his playing companions if he recognized his bounds and stayed within them. The safe way, though, leads to stagnation. Pain has no memory, and alienated players can be replaced if necessary. (It is prudent, however, to try to stay on good terms with cellists. Praise their tone and phrasing, and offer them the biggest piece of pie at refreshment time.) There are some fiendishly difficult passages even in works by Haydn and Mozart, e.g., the first violin part in the first movement of the Haydn Op. 76, No. 3 and the trio in the Mozart K589. As discussed below, composers from Beethoven on wrote for professional musicians without regard for the technical limitations of amateurs, and much of this music has rhythmic complexity and passages requiring near-virtuoso technique. Failure should be stimulus to improve, not discouragement.

Accommodating to the limitations of the quartet players in choosing what to play makes for more tranquil sessions and provides for little growth in ability. Trying a difficult work known only to the player who proposes it is often a cause of displays of bad temper because it increases the stress level. There is a resistance to the unknown approaching xenophobia, and some quartet players will start a work new to them reluctantly and refuse to play it further at the first set of problems encountered. Others will play through doggedly, complaining continually and uncivilly, playing some passages repeatedly until they sound reasonably good and agreeing to abandon others after a few attempts. After the new quartet has been attempted several times, the problems may be resolved, and the work will be one no longer feared by the players. (The caution has been stated that only one new work should be attempted during any one evening.)

In playing chamber music, as in any other activity, the first step in solving a problem is defining it. Sometimes the problem is conceptual — and looking at the score to see how the instruments relate, listening to a record made by a professional quartet or trying to play along with it may help. It is both instructive and frustrating to try to play a missing part with records designed for this. (It is convenient to transfer the record to tape, which can be controlled easier.) The frustration occurs in the realization that the three players on the record do not interact. If the first violin is the missing part, that player has to follow where normally the first leads. When the problems are solved to the extent that the "live" player finishes with the recorded ones, the frustration gives way to enjoyment. Sometimes the problem is mechanical; one simply cannot play so many notes at the indicated tempo in time and in tune. Working out fingering in slow tempo in individual practice and marking it on the part in pencil, followed by diligent practice, may resolve the problem. If one has time and funds to take lessons on the instrument, the teacher can be asked to help on a difficult passage. Not all problems are immediately soluble, but many are.

A favorite anecdote is the one where Samuel Johnson attended a violin recital with James Boswell. Boswell nudged the dozing Johnson and whispered, "What he is playing is exceedingly difficult." "Sir," was the retort, "I wish it were impossible." None of the chamber music literature is impossible for excellent players; some of it will be for many groups. Trying to play one difficult work in an evening to determine whether it is merely difficult or impossible at that time is worthwhile — providing all the players agree to the experiment. If there is a total breakdown, there is nothing to be done but agree to try again at some future time. If there is a partial failure, for instance a passage in which there are many notes above the staff with all kinds of accidentals, one that simply cannot be worked out without a great deal of study, the natural inclination is to cheat, to try to keep the tempo and hope the others are having problems there too and won't notice — or at least will not remark on it. A good ploy, if the cheating is detected and commented on, is to mention that one's prescription for eyeglasses at that range has to be strengthened. (Many players of mature years discover they need a special pair of spectacles for the distance to the music stand. For those with normal distance vision but decreased accommodation, an early and superseded pair of reading glasses might serve.)

Playing string quartets can be compared to an evening at bridge, where the players change partners. In both activities, there is a partnership between players, although the musicians change their relationships more often. As in bridge, it helps to have an insight into one's partner's habits of thought. In both, mistakes made by one player can lead to recriminations, unseemly verbal abuse and other sociopathic behavior patterns. (Unlike bridge, there are no records of a murder committed instigated by a playing blunder in amateur string quartets. Not that we would be surprised!) A tyro at chamber music may be pushed to and beyond his technical limits at certain points in the music, concentration on hitting the right notes leading to lapses in rhythm and an apparent disdain for dynamic markings. A colleague may yell out a "one" to signify the start of a measure, which is only sometimes helpful (which measure?), or a stentorian "pianissimo!" This often leads to complete destruction of concentration for the struggling player.

If a mistake by one player is treated intolerantly by any of the others, the player feels guilt and becomes defensive. Loss of self-confidence engenders further errors, and the enjoyment of the evening diminishes for everyone. It is much better simply to stop, then start again at a convenient measure number or letter, foregoing the ego-satisfaction of identifying the perpetrator. If the repetition is unsuccessful, then the problem can be identified by working out the passage with two players at a time, the others maintaining discreet silence. It should be accepted that each player is serious in intent, albeit sometimes deficient in execution. A "no fault" policy should obtain. A Rembrandt painting is not damaged if an art student draws a poor copy of it.

IX. Fiddling with Strangers

Get on a mailing list taken from the Amateur Chamber Music Players directory, and you will receive enticing brochures for chamber music weekends at hotels, for weeklong sessions at college campuses during the summer and for ocean cruises. Many of these offer artists-in-residence to provide inspiration and coaching, and opportunities to play with others at similar amateur levels enough for the most enthusiastic player. In addition, recreational facilities are made available in pleasant surroundings. Those on college campuses seem very reasonable in price, the chamber music groups serving to pay some of the overhead for the colleges during the months when no or few students are in residence. Amateurs may pay to play at chateaus on the Loire, Alpine lake resorts in Italy or castles in Hungary, combining touring and fiddling.

One participant in a chamber music week described the first meeting of a group of amateurs as a "sniffing session," like the first encounter between stray dogs. One summer, a viola player of considerable musical and intellectual accomplishment, persuaded her husband (a nonplayer) to join her at a college campus in Vermont for a chamber music vacation. While her mate surveyed the prospect of the surrounding Green Mountains and inventoried the tennis courts and other facilities, she was invited to sit in on a reading of the Mozart Clarinet Quintet. She had played it many times before, and she acquitted herself nobly. On the basis of this success, she was next conscripted by another amateur player, along with another woman, a staff cellist, to take part in the "Second Rasoumovsky," Beethoven's Op. 59, No. 2, in E minor.

She described "the first fiddle" later as a man with an imposing sense of authority—like that of corporation presidents and physicians—

who played the notes better than the music. Not an outstanding amateur player, but one whose playing reflected long experience and frequent practice. He set a pace faster than that adopted by most professionals. His playing was punctuated with imprecations at his companions, the most frequent of which was, "Wrong note!" There were several breakdowns in ensemble, increasing as the reading of the quartet continued. These allowed him to expatiate on his critique of his companions. The music ended with a spirited *Presto*; the two women ended in tears. The violist's husband found her crying in their room later. "Gee, I thought this was supposed to be a vacation!" he said. Years later, she had refused to play that quartet again, and she avoids attending recitals where it is programmed.

Most of the anecdotes provided in the ACMP newsletters about playing with strangers describe heroic efforts to arrange chamber music sessions by the host, incandescently fine playing and opulent surroundings and refreshments. These are not worth recounting; not only are they uninteresting, but they may lead to unrealistic expectations. One we enjoyed was a story of an American in Paris for whom a quartet was arranged. The first violin was a young woman who was a professional violinist. She continually chided the American for playing too loudly. At the end of the evening, the American mustered his schoolboy French to tell the first fiddle that it was an honor to play with her. Instead of "honneur," the word that came out was "horreur," perhaps a Freudian slip.

Writing about chamber music (in his painfully overblown style), Yehudi Menuhin described the string quartet as "...the highest form of musical activity...giving the purest musical satisfaction to those who play.... It is the expression of a cultivated society, of cultivated minds and refined spirits in human beings." Sir Yehudi knows a different group of players than we amateurs do.

X. Some Informative Reading

Reading Scores

It is always useful to read the scores of works that are to be played — if there is foreknowledge. It is also useful to review the scores of works that were played earlier, especially while memory of difficulties are fresh. Miniature scores are available for many chamber works, and Dover Books has published inexpensive collections of scores for the Haydn quartets; from Op. 20 through Op. 77, the complete Beethoven quartets, the complete Mozart quartets, complete Mozart quintets, and chamber music for strings of Schubert, Brahms, Schumann and Mendelssohn. It helps to have all the parts displayed so that interrelationships can be determined. These are also useful in fixing occasional errors printed in the parts. The player can develop facility in reading treble, viola, tenor and bass clefs with practice, but, even without this, reading scores is useful in establishing rhythmic interplay. Reading scores obviously is much easier than reading parts. Where scores are unavailable, the parts should be studied at points where difficulties were found.

Aulich and Heimeran

The little book by Bruno Aulich and Ernst Heimeran, *Das stillvergnügten Streichquartett*, was published by Ernst Heimeran Verlag, Munich, in 1936, and the English translation, augmented by the translator, D. Millar Craig, published in 1938 by H.W. Gray in Great Britain with the title, *The Well Tempered String Quartet*. A revised translation was published by Novello & Co., Ltd., in 1949. The book has chapters titled, "How a String Quartet comes into Being," "The Quartet Evening," "Now for Practice," "An Evening Performance," "All Around the String Quartet," a reprint of a newspaper article by Franz Anton Ledermann, a Berlin lawyer and amateur player (b. 1890) translated as "See You Again at the Double Bar, a Contribution to the Natural History of the Amateur Quartet," "Useful ABC" (a short and amusing glossary of musical terms) and appendices which exceed the length of the text, providing commentary on the literature of string quartets and other chamber music that quartet players may attempt. The translator provided much greater service than mere translation, serving to add comments on newer works and to update the coverage while maintaining the spirit of the original. "Translator" seems too modest a term, although the fine translation is not an inconsiderable feat. Added material is identified by a (T). The authors, and the translator, are entertaining and informative, and they have integrity, clearly identifying what is opinion.

Herter Norton

The Art of String Quartet Playing—Practice, Technique and Interpretation, by Mrs. M.D. Herter Norton, 1962, is available in paperback from W.W. Norton & Company, New York. This wonderful book is illustrated with 132 examples from scores, and it contains much wisdom and advice. As this writer's experience in quartet playing grows, he continually learns more from it. Of course, this is the paradox in books about playing music; the more you need them the less you understand their teachings. Writing about music has perils, even for superlatively trained people like Mrs. Norton. Discussing dynamics, she observed that a forte in Haydn or Mozart should not be as loud as in "Brahms, the red-blooded." What the hematocrit of the composer has to do with the loudness with which his quartets are played eludes us. No musicologist has written that either Haydn or Mozart was anemic. We play *fortes* loud all the time, not to mention our complaints about the volume of *piano* from our fellows.

Rosemary Hughes

A slim book by Rosemary Hughes, *Haydn String Quartets*, BBC Publications, London, 1966, is another that repays reading and rereading. It gives information on the provenance of the quartets and many examples from score. The same author has a book in The Master Musicians series published by J.M. Dent & Co., Ltd., London (revised 1977), and titled, *Haydn*, with a wealth of information on his life and his works in all forms, including a chapter on his chamber music for strings. Haydn shared the same year of birth, 1732, with George Washington, and nothing bad can be said of either great man. The life of Haydn could be held as an exemplar even to the tone-deaf. With humble origins, thrown on his own resources at an early age, he lived to age 77. Like Washington, he left no children. Washington became known as Father of His Country, and Haydn is still called Papa Haydn. Haydn's genius enriched his generation and all that followed. He was hard-working, reverent, generous and loyal. Haydn was one of those singular souls who achieved his potential.

Ruttencutter

Quartet; A Profile of the Guarneri Quartet was published in part in *The New Yorker* by Helen Drees Ruttencutter, and the expanded book edition was published by Lippincott and Crowell, New York, 1980. This is a fascinating description of the activities of a preëminent professional quartet. Comparing professional string quartets with each other is a valid cocktail party activity among music lovers. It is done explicitly by music critics and implicitly by concert ticket buyers. It is futile and frustrating for most amateurs to try to compare what it is they do with how world-class professional string quartets play. The operative verb in most juxtapositions of professional and amateur, whatever the field, is contrast, not compare.

The Strad

A monthly journal called *The Strad,* published by Novello in the United Kingdom, carries many articles about quartet players and string quartets as well as reviews of concerts, records and new editions of sheet music. Some of the profiles of British musicians bring to mind Shaw's phrase, "fawning over fiddlers," and there are occasional gratuitous attacks on "Hollywood hotshot fiddlers" (presumably, Americans in general), in limning the virtues of the honest yeoman fiddlers of Britain, ever ready to flex their bows in defense of the Sceptered Isle if Agincourt occurs again. All the same, the British flavor has charm. The journal has lasted many decades. In recent years, it has become more international in scope and less parochial in its editorial attitudes. Issues over the past several years have featured illustrations in color.

Strings

The first volume of *Strings* was first published in 1986. This is a quarterly, published by the String Letter Corporation of San Anselmo, California. It has articles on playing, instrument makers, and auction prices.

Chamber Music

The quarterly magazine of Chamber Music America, an organization for professionals which amateurs may join as associate members, is called simply *Chamber Music*.

Paul Griffiths

Paul Griffiths' *The String Quartet: A History,* Thames and Hudson, New York, 1983, is a good reference on string quartet music from its inception to close to the book's publication date. Like most books on music, it takes on the impossible task of describing one art with another. It is, in general, comparable to writing a book on painting without illustrations. One scans such books for passages about works that are familiar and checks off concurrence or disagreement with the author's judgments. Nevertheless, this is worthwhile as a reference as well as for the opinions expressed.

Alexander Hyatt-King

Mozart Chamber Music, by A. Hyatt-King is a slim paperback, published by BBC, London, 1968, with good information on the history of Mozart's compositions in this genre and some examples from score. It provides a useful table of K numbers.

Hans Keller

The estimable Hans Keller has provided an interesting analysis of the great Haydn quartets—*The Great Haydn Quartets; Their Interpretation,* J.M. Dent & Sons, Ltd., London, 1986. The 18 page preface is fascinating, but the analysis of the quartets requires more knowledge of musical subtleties than this reader yet possesses. Of the 83 Haydn quartets published by Peters, those of Op. 3 are now considered dubious in authorship, and Op. 51, "The Seven Last Words of Christ," is counted as seven quartets, leaving 70 quartets to choose among. Keller selected 45 and the unfinished Op. 103 as the great quartets. His choices are tabulated below:

Op.	No.	Op.	No.	Op.	No.	Op.	No.	Op.	No.	Op.	No.
9	4	20	1	20	2	20	3	20	4	20	5
20	6	33	1	33	2	33	3	33	5	33	6
42	—	50	1	50	2	50	3	50	4	50	5
50	6	54	1	54	2	54	3	55	1	55	2
55	3	64	1	64	2	64	3	64	4	64	5
64	6	71	1	71	2	71	3	74	1	74	2
74	3	76	1	76	2	76	3	76	4	76	5
76	6	77	1	77	2	103	—				

Keller did not have the problem faced by Moser and Dechert for Peters, selecting only 30 quartets to be "celebrated." A comparison shows that Keller omits Op. 9, No. 2, and Op. 17, No. 5, and the two Op. 3 quartets, accepting 26 of the 30 anointed by the Peters editors. Selecting 30 of the most beautiful and representative Haydn quartets would make an interesting parlor game for amateur chamber music players who are familiar with all of the quartets. Comparing lists would make for some fascinating bar room discussions.

Hans Keller's chapter on Mozart's chamber music in *The Mozart Companion* (H.C. Robbins Landon and Donald Mitchell, editors), Oxford University Press, New York, 1956, is worthwhile both for its information and ascerbic viewpoints. Keller expressed low regard for the early quartets as poor imitations of Haydn. Mozart's chamber music with flute showed how little the composer liked that instrument, while his chamber music with clarinet showed the opposite.

Homer Ulrich

Ulrich provided a scholarly treatise on the music, not on the playing of it — *Chamber Music; The Growth and Practice of an Intimate Art,* Columbia University Press, New York, 1948. Not until the 8th chapter, of 13, does his chronology reach Haydn.

Charles Rosen

The Classical Style by Charles Rosen, Viking Press, New York, 1971, is a splendid contribution by a noted pianist, a man with great gifts in the art of exposition in English prose as well as at his keyboard. This book may well become a classic. Its author examined the works of Haydn, Mozart and Beethoven, and there are searching analyses of Haydn's string quartets and piano trios and of Mozart's string quintets as primary examples of the composer's work. One striking insight provided explained the predominance of the string quartet. According to Rosen, classical composers obtained dramatic effect by dissonance on a triad, thus four players were required. Accomplishing this with a trio requires techniques such as double-stopping and rapid note-changing. Using more than four players engenders problems in doubling and balances. In a discussion of the Haydn piano trios, the author points out that the piano and violin have developed greater volume than the instruments available in the last part of the 18th century, so that the balances are different. Although the classical piano could provide the harmonic and melodic lines by itself, its bass line was weak and was augmented by the cello. The modern violin set-up, with strengthened bass bar, lengthened finger board at a different angle, and the use of vibrato, is another change from classical practice. Thus, the classical composers wrote for the sounds that were possible in their era.

W.W. Cobbett

Cobbett's Cyclopedic Survey of Chamber Music is a British publication in three volumes. The first two were published in 1929 by Oxford University Press, London, edited by Walter Willson Cobbett. The third, a supplement was published in 1963, with Colin Mason as editor. It provides a critical analysis of composers of chamber music and some of their works.

Grove Dictionary

The New Grove Dictionary of Music and Musicians, edited by Stanley Sadie, is a 20-volume reference published in 1980 by Macmillan of London and Grove's Dictionaries of Music, Inc., of Washington, D.C. Articles on composers are followed by lists of their works in categories, Chamber Works being one. This would be tremendously impressive in an amateur's music room, but its cost sends us to our nearest public library.

ACMP Lists

The ACMP publishes lists of recommended chamber music at intervals, the tenth list having been provided to members in 1988. The lists include comments and assessments of difficulty where these have been provided by members, along with the names of publishers and agents for publishers. Lists of holdings in the Helen Rice collection, available for loan from the Hartford (Connecticut) Library, are provided. In addition to ACMP services, membership and its consequent listing brings advertisements from instrument dealers, book publishers and sheet music sellers. It is ego-building to be offered a rare antique violin at a price exceeding that of your home in the same mail delivery as the telephone bill.

Melvin Berger

Berger's *Guide to Chamber Music* Dodd, Mead, New York, 1985, provides a description of music by many composers, including contemporaries. It is organized alphabetically by composer name, and it includes background information on the composers and their works along with descriptions of quartets, trios, woodwind music and works with piano. It was disheartening to find discussions only of the Haydn "Celebrated Quartets."

Altmann

Wilhelm Altmann's *Kammermusik -Katalog* provides a comprehensive listing of the chamber music literature, provided one accepts that it was first published more than 50 years ago. An unchanged reprint of the book was published by Hofmeister, Hofheim am Ts., in 1965. The amateur quartet player soon learns that literature available varies with time and with country.

An Apologia

We have provided only a sampling of books and periodicals available. Some readers might have wanted us to provide an exhaustive bibliography or a critique of the literature on chamber music. For the first task, we plead lack of motivation. For the second, lack of expert qualifications. Although we hesitate not a bit in providing opinions, these are presented with the caveat that they come from an informed amateur with dubious talent as a chamber musician. Those inclined to intellectual analysis of their leisure activity will need no stimulus to explore the music sections of libraries and book stores. The "invincible ignoramuses" who do not care about the composers and the origins of their works will not read. Those of us in the first category — the writer and readers of this volume — will develop enough judgment through playing that we can read critically.

Authority of the Written Word

One time the writer proposed playing a Haydn quaratet that is not in the "celebrated" volumes. The host went immediately to his bookshelf to see if Aulich and Heimeran approved before he agreed. It would show more self-assurance (or arrogance) to play the quartet first, form an opinion, then determine if Aulich and Heimeran were "correct" in their opinion. These were, after all, amateur players. Professional players have — or should have — impeccable technique, but comparison of their writings and statements in interviews show they differ among themselves in matters of intelligence and taste. Some, like Rosen mentioned above, provide illumination. The statements and writings produced by others of them are painfully fatuous. After all, if high sensibility and great culture were the requisites for playing superbly, we, the writer and readers of this book, would be the envy of our quartet-playing companions.

XI. Composers and Decomposers

One quartet player describes his experience with the statement that he has played the music of "every dead composer" as well as many of the more modern who use a tonal idiom. This would be a magnificent accomplishment were it true, but it is hyperbole. While the literature of string quartets in print is vast, only approached in size by that of piano trios, a large portion of it is out of print. Bachman's *Encyclopedia of the Violin,* published in the 1920s, lists two quartets by Zdeněk Fibich (1850–1900) and eight by Joachim Raff (1822–82) along with six quartets by Anton Rubinstein (1829–94) and many others with less familiar names. (Fibich and Raff are evocative of violin pieces played in my youth, "Poème" and "Cavatina," respectively; Rubinstein of the "Melody in F.") Ignaz Pleyel (1757–1831) wrote 45 string quartets; occasionally, a flute quartet or duo is heard.

Boccherini (1743–1805) produced dozens of string quartets and more than 100 string quintets, of which only a few are currently in print. Louis Spohr (1784–1859) published 34 string quartets, four double quartets, a sextet and an octet. Few of these are heard, although a Heifetz recording of one of the double quartets is occasionally broadcast. Darius Milhaud (1892–1974) wrote 18 string quartets, of which the 14th and 15th were written to be performed separately or played together as an octet. (There is a story about a recording session where the Budapest String Quartet undertook the octet version, first recording one quartet then the other while equipped with headphones. Boris Kroyt, the violist, grumbled that he could have done six of the parts all by himself.)

Only a small fraction of the output of dead composers remains in print. Not all the quartets of living composers are available. Undoubtedly, much of what lies buried in the limbo of "out-of-print" deserves its obscurity, but some diamonds must gleam unnoticed among the coals. It is saddening to think of people like Anton Rubinstein who were acclaimed in their time, remembered now — if at all — by a salon piece. Rubinstein was famous as a pianist and teacher along with his brother. He toured the United States with Henri Wieniawski, the violin virtuoso, presenting 215 concerts in eight months! He published 10 string quartets among a large body of work in many forms. (Perhaps these are played in the USSR; they appear to be unplayed and unavailable in listings in the United States. A player in the Taneyev Quartet from Leningrad complained that most American quartets, e.g., those by Ives, are unavailable in his country.) A sampling of monthly program listings of a classical music radio station shows not one of his compositions. One may hear a beautiful string quartet broadcast — the Glazounov Op. 70, No. 5, is an example — and search in vain for the music. (The recording was by the Leningrad Philharmonic Quartet.) Only small portions of the work of other once-renowned composers are presented in broadcasts. Perhaps the law of survival of the fittest has prevailed. There is no way to determine this without searching music archives.

Sources of Quartet Parts

How, then, does the amateur quartet find music to play? If it is not available for purchase or loan, there is no way to play it. One must visit stores that sell sheet music and consult lists. Personal inspection of stocks of music in a store is preferable. One can make a judgment on whether or not the music is playable at his quartet's level and see the price. The amateur quartet-player in a music store is a gourmand at a candy counter. Music is available more conveniently from lists and mail order catalogs, and the amateur may choose from these. Reading through parts and hearing what they sound like in the mind is a skill beyond most amateurs.

Very often, the selection of music is based on having heard it at a concert, on a broadcast or on recordings. Sometimes, the choice is made on the basis of knowledge of another quartet by the same composer. One who has enjoyed playing the Dvořák "American" quartet might well want to buy all of the quartets by him that are available. Familiarity with works of the composer in other forms might prompt a search for string quartets he wrote. Anton Arensky (1861–1906) wrote a warm, romantic piano trio which is often heard in concert and recordings. A search for his quartets, one of which is the source of his "Variations on a Theme of Tchaikovsky"—occasionally heard in an orchestral version—is likely to be unrewarding. Books describing quartet literature provide the more-or-less informed opinion of their authors. That a work may be in the author's library does not guarantee that it is still available for sale.

Gerald Abraham, describing a Russian conception of chamber music, wrote of "music to be enjoyed by players not quite of the first rank rather than listened to by intellectuals with their heads in their hands." The image suggests that these two are mutually exclusive. (I quote out of context in admiration for the phrase.) The amateur string quartet generally is technique-limited, but its members may be head-in-hands intellectuals. They enjoy playing masterpieces. This is all to the good, because only masterpieces are readily available and relatively inexpensive.

On the other hand, there are 20th century quartets which seem to be written for musicologists. (Someone defined a musicologist derisively as a scholar who knows all there is to know about music—and hates the sound of it.) Some of these cannot be considered modern any longer. The tone row compositions of Schoenberg and his followers, for example, have been available for most of the century. Audiences listen respectfully, trying to understand the idiom, but many of us have given up on these as a special case of head-in-hands music; hands over ears. Many contemporary composers complain that their work has no audience. When they write chamber music on commission from a professional group, it may get few performances. Concert managers have a decisive influence on program content.

Amateur players constitute a very sophisticated audience for music. For more than 50 years, they have sat politely and respectfully listening to atonal and serial music—and few have learned to appreciate it. A practical consideration in the amateur string quartet is the problem of identifying errors in playing atonal music. Other composers of our time have written music which amateurs enjoy playing, e.g.,

Barber, Shostakovich and Hindemith. The great increase in popularity of professional chamber music in the second half of this century may well lead to a larger repertory of contemporary works for amateurs. Recognition of the potential market in amateur string quartets might elicit revival of some 19th century works that have disappeared from publishers' lists. The idea of "music to be enjoyed by players not quite of the first rank," even if not profound, is attractive to amateurs.

The string quartet medium affords the almost vocal expressiveness of the violin family, with their protean tonal effects, along with the limitations of using but four similar instruments. The transparency of the string quartet, illuminating each of the four lines, leaves little room for hiding shoddy workmanship and pedestrian ideas for works that extend from about 15 minutes to about 45 minutes. Many of the great composers met the challenge of these restrictions and produced their best work in this medium. Most amateur quartets now play the music of "dead composers" practically exclusively, but amateurs played their music while these composers were contemporaries.

Composers in Their Own Times

Haydn (1732–1809) enjoyed a good income from sales of his quartets in his later years; Mozart (1756–1791) and Schubert (1797–1828) well might have also — but they had no later years. These were days before copyright, and composers made arrangements with one or more music publishers. (Fortunately for them, they antedated invention of xerographic copiers and computers.) The composer, thus, had a versatile and expressive medium for ideas with the potential of money coming in on publication. The purchasers of the editions of quartets had a convenient number of players to assemble — sometimes this could be kept within the family — and the material for countless evenings of recreation.

Some wit wrote about an apocryphal tone-deaf efficiency expert who studied a symphony orchestra. The expert's report had recommendations for decreasing the number of violins, violas and cellos on the basis that the two violin sections each had several players of the same music and nearly all in the others were redundant. The report noted that wind and percussion players spent a great amount of time waiting to play, and it suggested that players in these sections learn to play several of the instruments, and that composers and arrangers should facilitate this versatility by keeping these functionaries busy a substantial portion of the time. The efficiency expert would have no quarrel with the string quartet, a marvel of cost-effectiveness.

From the player's standpoint, the home string quartet is very nearly the perfect medium for enjoyment; the number of players is comfortable, the music available is sublime and the challenges without end. Thus the form has endured for more than 200 years, and contemporary composers continue to enrich the literature. Nevertheless, Pierre Boulez (1925–), a renowned French composer and conductor, was quoted, just before the chamber music boom occurred in the United States, as saying that he intended to rework his early string quartet composition in a different medium because the string quartet is a defunct art form. Aside from weakening his credentials as a prophet, does this qualify him as a "decomposer?"

Intellectual Pretension

Listening to chamber music developed a curious reputation as the province of intellectuals some time during the 19th century. This persisted through the middle of the 20th. Brahms, especially, was regarded as cerebral, which would no doubt have amused this erstwhile bawdy house pianist. The subsidization of string quartets by university music schools as artists in residence, with free recitals in the university community, exposed large numbers of people to the beauties of chamber music, and its audience grew. (The first university-sponsored quartet in the United States was established in 1940: the Pro Arte String Quartet at the University of Wisconsin. The Pro Arte was founded in Belgium in the 1920s, but it was led at Wisconsin by the Austrian, Rudolf Kolisch. The second university string quartet was established after World War II at the University of California, led by Sidney Griller. Many universities in the United States and other countries followed the lead of these magnificent communities of scholars.)

Like all art forms, chamber music does have an intellectual component, but it can be and is enjoyed on many levels. It is rich in melody, harmony, rhythm and invention. Playing it, or trying to play it, is a magnificent way to learn it. Knowing something about the origins of the music adds to the enjoyment of both players and listeners. Not all listeners are players, but players must be listeners. It cannot be denied that listening to chamber music is an esoteric taste. A survey of the enormous parking lot of The Grand Old Opry in Nashville shows cars registered in every state and nearly every Canadian province, their passengers having come to sit in an auditorium holding more than 5000 people for each performance of country music. Audiences for chamber music performances are much smaller. We like to think of ourselves as an elite in taste and refinement. It is a harmless conceit.

The Repertory

What is played by amateur string quartets depends on the players' abilities, their libraries of music and their preferences. Sometimes, the group as a whole will have a plan for playing music in some sequence. Several years ago, teams of quartet players at the University of Wisconsin performed the feat of playing all of Haydn quartets in one marathon session. Occasionally, one player will set himself a goal such as playing the first violin part for all of the quartets in a Haydn volume in the order they appear, one per evening. Again, someone will suggest a quartet on the basis of having heard it at a concert or on a broadcast, and someone may have practiced and annotated a part.

In the course of one recent calendar year when his goal of averaging one chamber music session per week was realized, this writer played first violin, second and viola at various times; occasionally all three during an evening. (The majority of the evenings were devoted to string quartets, but some of them were string quintets and trios, piano trios and quartets, and piano-violin sonatas. These were noted, but they are not listed here.) Quartet players, other than the writer, totaled 22 during the year. (This compares well with the 20 given earlier as a good number for a list.) Of these 22, nine people played first, six played second, seven played viola and seven cello. (The total of 29 reflects the fact that several people play both violin and viola. One played violin, viola and cello.) The quartets played during that year are listed below, with the number of times played in parenthesis:

Beethoven Op. 18, No. 1 (4), No. 2 (2), No. 3 (1), No. 4 (3), No. 5 (3), No. 6 (2); Op. 59, No. 1 (1), No. 2 (2), No. 3 (5); Op. 130 (1), Op. 131 (1), Op. 132 (1)

Borodin No. 1 (1), No. 2 (2)

Brahms Op. 51, No. 2 (2); Op. 67 (1)

Debussy Op. 10 (1)

Dvořák Op. 34 (3); Op 51 (1); Op. 96 (2)

Glazounov Op. 26 (1)

Haydn Op. 9, No. 2 (1); Op. 17, No. 5 (1), No. 6 (1); Op. 20, No. 2 (2), No. 3 (3), No. 5 (1); Op. 33, No. 1 (1), No. 3 (2); Op. 42 (2); Op. 50, No. 1 (1), No. 2 (2), No. 3 (1), No. 4 (1), No. 5 (1), No. 6 (2); Op. 54, No. 1 (1); Op. 55, No. 1 (2), No. 3 (1); Op. 64, No. 5 (2), No. 6 (3); Op. 71, No. 2 (1), No. 3 (2); Op. 74, No. 1 (2), No. 2 (1); Op. 76, No. 1 (4), No. 2 (3), No. 3 (1), No. 5 (3); Op. 77, No. 1 (3); Op. 103 (1)

Joplin Rags (transcription) (1)

Mendelssohn Op. 12 (1); Op. 13 (2); Op. 44, No. 1 (1)

Mozart K387 (5), K428 (1), K458 (4), K464 (4), K465 (2), K499 (2), K546 (1), K575 (3), K589 (2), K590 (2)

Schubert No. 7 in D (1), No. 9 in G Minor (5), No. 12 in C Minor (5), No. 13 in A Minor (1), No. 14 in D Minor (2), No. 15 in G (1)

Schumann Op. 41, No. 1 (2), No. 2 (2)

Shostakovich No. 1 in C (1)

Smetana No. 1 in E Minor (1)

Thus, during one calendar year, this writer played 74 string quartets, several more than once. (Other players may have played more or fewer, since the composition of the quartet varied.) Virtually all of them are standard works of the great composers. The reason for this is discussed elsewhere, but may be summarized as: only proven masterpieces are readily available at reasonable cost. There are many examples like Anton Rubinstein—composers who wrote and published many quartets, none of which are listed in catalogs by music publishers. Without ever having heard these, we can guess that they show a certain level of competence. There follows a chronological survey of the great composers of chamber music.

Franz Josef Haydn (1732–1809)

Haydn was a towering genius. He had a prodigious output of compositions in all forms: operas, symphonies, concerti, oratorios and others as well as chamber music. When Robert Schumann showed his own three quartets of Op. 41 to his wife, he announced "they were as good as Haydn's." At that time, Schumann knew the string quartets of Mozart, Beethoven, Schubert, Mendelssohn and many others, but Haydn was his criterion of greatness in the medium. Amateur quartets often decide to begin their evening by "warming up" with a Haydn quartet "and move ahead." What should be inferred is that they will move ahead chronologically, not musically. Other composers were as prolific as Haydn — Boccherini and Johann Wanhal (1739–1813), both with 100 quartets — but no one else produced as many masterpieces in the form.

Haydn did not invent the string quartet, but he is justifiably called its father because of his development of it. None of his contemporaries provided any quartets of comparable quality until Mozart produced the six quartets he dedicated to Haydn. A chronology of technology shows a continual development, so that the computer is a significant advance on the typewriter, which was in turn an advance on the pen, the goose quill and the stylus. No such advance can be traced in string quartet-writing. Arguably, the instruments and instrumental technique have improved, although there are advocates of "authentic" instruments and styles. Certainly, different forms of music have evolved since the classical epoch which Haydn contributed to; the romantic, the atonal and tone row styles, and influences of sources other than folk musics, such as jazz. Quite naturally, music since the time of Haydn has been different from his. The professional string quartet as a "play for pay"organization began in the 19th century. Composers were thus liberated from the constraint of writing works amenable to amateur levels of technique. The romantic epoch in music also liberated composers from conventions such as sonata form and the rigid relationship among keys and harmonies. Given the resources at his disposal and the conventions of his time, Haydn produced miracle upon miracle. G.B. Shaw's preface to *Caesar and Cleopatra* asked the question, "Better than Shakespeare?," comparing himself to a playwright who lived nearly 300 years earlier. Can one fairly ask if Schumann or Shostakovich is better than Haydn? It is an unanswerable question. All we can conclude is that later composers were different, writing music of their times, not Haydn's.

The string quartet as an art form is more than merely music scored for two violins, a viola and a cello. Music was written for this combination of instruments before Haydn. For the most part, it was music for serenades or background, where the string quartet functioned as a string orchestra reduced to the minimum. The popular *Eine kleine Nachtmusik* of Mozart (K525) was a late example, a suite of pleasant tunes which can be played by a quartet, is better with a double bass added and best with a string orchestra. The 12 quartets of Haydn's Op. 1 and Op. 2 are pieces of this type, mostly two fast outer movements, two minuet-trio movements and a slow movement in the center. Even here, Haydn showed evidence of experimenting with form. With the Op. 9 and Op. 17, he grappled with the expression of profound ideas in the medium, and he continued to do so throughout his creative life.

Haydn was a wonderful human being. His contribution to music may be compared with Shakespeare's to English literature. Born in an Austrian village, the son of a wheelwright, he showed musical talent as a young child. He learned the elements of music in 10 years as a boy soprano in the choir of St. Stephen's Church in Vienna, and he was literally thrown out at age 18 (!) when his voice broke. (This characteristic of late maturation persisted.) For a while, he subsisted by giving music lessons to children, then he became assistant music director for Count Morzin. In 1761, he became music director for the princely Esterházy family, responsible for producing compositions of all types. His status was that of a servant, but he had resources of instrument players and singers available to him. He taught himself composition, and he never stopped developing ideas during his long life. From the study of his compositions—even the casual study that comes from playing them—one can infer that he was continually experimenting.

Haydn had an unhappy and childless marriage, which may account to some extent for the time he spent working. He worked with great self-discipline and devotion. He became famous in his own lifetime, and his personality was such that his recognition evoked little jealously or enmity from his contemporaries. In the sense that Haydn was father of the string quartet, he is recognized as father of the symphony, 104 being the usual number of these given. Haydn wrote some beautiful piano trios, but the limitations of the instruments available at the time dictated that the cello parts doubled the bass of the piano. Probably, the lack of challenge to cellists limits their performances, but they contain wonderful ideas. His concertos for cello are staples of the concert repertory, leaving no doubt he knew how to write effectively for that instrument. One infers that he was more concerned with the effect of the whole work instead of the equality of division of parts. One of the Esterházy princes played the baryton, a leg viol with bowed and sympathetic strings. His dutiful servant wrote 126 trios for baryton, even learning how to play it at the urging of his master. (Reportedly, the noble's nose was put out of joint when Haydn showed too much skill at it.) He wrote many operas, but the outmoded conventions of the time preclude hearing many performances of them. Overall, it is not extravagant to claim that Haydn was a major contributor to our civilization.

Influence of and on Haydn. Haydn's quartet production extended over 50 years, and he showed continual growth in the medium. It is not always recognized that Haydn's quartets from about his Op. 54 on were published after all of Mozart's and that his last was contemporaneous with Beethoven's Op. 18. What is remarkable about Haydn, expecially in view of his prolific output, is that each of the quartets is original, differing from all others. There is much greater difference in form, mood and spirit, for instance, among the six quartets of Haydn's Op. 76, all written about the same time, than among the six Mendelssohn (1809–1846) quartets that were published.

It is well-documented that Haydn and Mozart had mutual admiration and great influence on each other. Many writers on these great composers divide their discussion of Haydn's quartets in two groups, one ending with Op. 33 which inspired Mozart's great contributions, and the second beginning after these were published. There is logic to this. All chamber music players and other lovers of music enjoy a legacy from mutual respect and admiration of Haydn and Mozart. An often quoted aphorism credited to (or blamed on) Ernest Walker is, "Haydn first showed Mozart how to write string quartets; Mozart then showed Haydn how string quartets should be written." The quote is facile, but it is odious to an admirer of Haydn. Haydn, working long and thoughtfully, taught himself and posterity how string quartets should be written, developing the medium from its infancy and continually trying new approaches.

Haydn's works, then, are the foundation of an amateur string quartet library. All of the quartets demand a competent—and sometimes virtuosic—first violin, but the earlier ones require less technical ability from the other three players. Nevertheless, they are always interesting. Haydn's work is full of humor and unexpected resolutions. It provides enjoyment and enrichment for the rank amateur and the advanced player. The more one plays Haydn, the more respect and love is developed for the composer. Haydn lived in a time and a culture when a musician was a servant of the nobility. He was expected to provide music for all occasions, serve as an instrumentalist when needed, and direct the musicians assigned to him. He had resources provided for his art, but he worked under the strictures of an employee, dependent on the approval of his prince for his livelihood until he was nearly 60 years old.

Luigi Boccherini (1743–1805)

Boccherini was cosmopolitan as well as prolific. He was born in Italy and died in Spain. At one time he was court composer for Friedrich Wilhelm II in Berlin. In addition to 100 string quartets, he wrote more than 100 string quintets and a few quintets for guitar and quartet. Two collections of "representative"quartets are available in the United States. Those we have played are pleasant, and they are characteristic and similar to each other.

Wolfgang Amadeus Mozart (1756-1791)

Mozart attempted to break free of the employee relationship customary for composers of his time by living from sales of his music; however, he died impoverished before his 36th birthday. (His genius at music did not carry over to his skills at gambling.) Mozart's quartets can be divided into the early works (14 quartets) and 10 that were composed from K387 on. (The "K" numbers derive from Ludwig von Köchel (1800–1877), an Austrian scientist who provided a chronological thematic catalog of the composer's output in 1862.)

The earlier quartets are not very interesting, although some of the movements foreshadow the genius that developed. (Keller remarked that Mozart was a genius, but he was not a prodigy.) The six quartets designated K387, 421, 428, 458, 464 and 465 are the quartets dedicated to Haydn. These are interesting to all the players, with the K421 having an especially fine viola solo. Among these quartets, the K464, in A, was Beethoven's favorite—his Op. 18, No. 5, uses it as a model. K499 stands by itself. This quartet, in D, is sometimes called "The Hoffmeister" after the publisher and composer. The last three quartets, K475, K489 and K490, were dedicated to King Friedrich Wilhelm II of Prussia, a cellist, and they are often called the Prussian Quartets. According to Keller, the Germans call these "solo quartets," because Mozart solved the problem of writing a prominent cello part for the king by giving each of the instruments solo passages. The Adagio and Fugue, K546, was a work by Mozart in which he transcribed an earlier fugue for two pianos and prefixed a new adagio. This is a masterpiece which should not be overlooked by the home quartet player. Few of the mature Mozart—or later Haydn—quartets are difficult for amateurs to get through technically, although musical interpretation could require prolonged study. No one but the players themselves should have to suffer from these ad hoc efforts.

Ludwig van Beethoven (1770-1827)

Beethoven published chamber music, namely three piano trios, as his Opus 1 in 1795. (I once remarked to a coworker that I could not arrange a quartet, so I was playing piano trios that evening. She looked at me in distress and puzzlement and asked, "How do you get three pianos in your house?" After I recovered my composure, I explained that a piano trio is a piano, violin and cello and that such a grouping is next to string quartets in popularity. Further, I explained, it is usual to name a mixed group by the "hetero" instrument, thus a clarinet quintet is a work for clarinet and string quartet. She was sorry she asked.) His first set of six quartets was published in 1801 as Op. 18. (Haydn's Op. 103, an unfinished work for which only the middle two movements were completed, was published in 1803.)

These early Beethoven quartets follow most of the conventions of the age. (It was noted above that No. 5 was modeled after Mozart's K464 in its key signature and arrangement.) These are within the competence range of the beginning string quartet player, although they are not written to be as comfortable to the players as were the Haydn and Mozart quartets. The so-called Middle Quartets comprise the three of Op. 59, composed in 1806, and the Op. 74 (1809) and Op. 95 (1810). By this time the composer had obtained the patronage of Viennese nobility, who provided him with an annual stipend and the use of a quartet of professional musicians. These quartets give evidence that Beethoven no longer was restricted to the technical ability of amateur players, being independent of income from their purchase of his music, and he was even unsympathetic to complaints of technical difficulty by the professional players. (Beethoven's subsidy fell victim to the financial collapse of Austria, and he became dependent on money from publishers, but he was a hero in his own time and did well.)

Amateurs can play the "middle" quartets, but, by the time beginners master them, they qualify as veterans. The late-period quartets date from 1824 and comprise Op. 127, Op. 130, Op. 131, Op. 132, Op. 133 and Op. 135. Opus 133, the "Grosse Fuge," was written as the last movement of the six-movement Op. 130, but the publisher objected to its length. Because of this, Beethoven wrote a substitute last movement, and the great fugue was published separately; he was completely deaf when these were written. These quartets give all the players great challenges. They require much study for the listener and even more for the player. Here, Beethoven established his own forms. It requires much effort to get through these technically and still more to make music — but it is worth the effort to get inside the music.

Franz Schubert (1797–1828)

Schubert is credited with 15 string quartets, many of them beloved of amateurs and professionals alike. Only one of them was published in his brief lifetime, and opus numbers, where there are any, do not correspond to dates of composition. His works were provided a chronological catalog by Otto Erich Deutsch (1883–1967) in 1951, and they have D numbers (similar to the K numbers of Mozart's work). Deutsch was a prominent Austrian musicologist, who fled the Nazis in 1939, became a British subject and returned to Vienna several years after World War II. He also wrote on Haydn, Mozart, Handel, Schumann and Beethoven.

Schubert's genius was recognized ten years after his death, when Schumann, in his role as editor of a music journal, championed his music. Some of his songs enjoyed popularity during his lifetime, but he realized little profit from them. Most of his best loved quartets, including the "Death and the Maiden," D810 (the 14th) and the *Quartettsatz* (or quartet movement), D703 (the 12th) were posthumous publications. Alfred Einstein cited a letter Schubert wrote to his brother Ferdinand, stating that the family quartet should play other people's quartets instead of his early ones, as a repudiation by the composer of his early work. He might have felt disheartened or humble on the day he wrote the letter. Perhaps he tried to evoke a reply of "Nonsense, beloved brother, we love to play your works."

Unlike Brahms, Schubert did not destroy his early works. Amateur quartet players do not repudiate them to this day. The 8th quartet, D112, like most of Schubert's work has beautiful themes; however, it is a "first violin quartet," with that instrument getting most of the melody and the others mostly providing accompaniment. The 9th quartet, D173 in G Minor, shows an immense advance, being rewarding for all the players. It is a favorite in the ITSQ. The quartets in E♭, and E have moments of beauty, but they are prolix and pedestrian in large part compared with the works that followed. The *Quartettsatz*, No. 12 in C Minor, is a powerful and beautiful quartet movement, difficult only for the first violin but enjoyable for all the players. (We have an image of Schubert writing his quartets on tablecloths in a Viennese cafe, and we blame some overzealous bus boy for putting the remaining movements of this one in the wash. There is no historical basis for this fancy, but we are reluctant to permit fact to interfere with whimsy.)

The remaining quartets are masterpieces of the quartet literature. The A Minor quartet employs a theme used both in Schubert's Rosamunde music and in a piano impromptu in the *Andante* movement. This is the only one of the great quartets to have been published during Schubert's life. The D Minor quartet, D810, uses the theme from *Tod und das Mädchen* (Death and the Maiden), in a magnificent theme and variations Andante in G Minor. (I never play this quartet without thinking of the time I was presented with two tickets to hear the Guarneri in New York. My wife had a previous engagement, and we agreed that I should offer to take our son, then about 16. He responded to the invitation with, "Sure, Dad, I've never heard a *real* string quartet." Death and the Maiden was the high point of the program for him. We devoted amateur players develop hides tough enough to withstand barbs hurled even by our near and dear ones.) The last quartet, D887, is long, difficult, dramatic and glorious. The Schubert quartets from D703 on are all individual masterpieces of the literature, and all of the players have interesting parts. Because they are so long, there is more than the usual tendency to ignore repeat markings.

Juan Crisóstomo de Arriaga (1802–1822)

Arriaga was a Spanish prodigy who died of consumption before his 20th birthday. Among other works, he left three quartets, which are melodious and have challenges for all the players. The first of these, in D Minor, is a favorite, but all three are gratifying.

Felix Mendelssohn (1809–1846)

Mendelssohn was said to have been born a genius and died a talent. He was a member of a prominent family. His grandfather, Moses, was a great Jewish philosopher. His father, Abraham, was a wealthy banker, who converted the family to Lutheran protestantism. Abraham lamented that he was known for being the son of his father in his youth and the father of his son in his maturity.

Felix was a wealthy man who enjoyed success in his music, recognition by his public and peers and happiness in his home life. Unfortunately, he died young. His quartets may be more satisfying for the players than listeners. Opus 13 in A Minor was the first written, and it among the most satisfying. Opus 12 in E♭, features a *Canzonetta* that has the charm of a salon piece. Opus 44, No. 1, in D overdoes the tremelo accompaniments, and the drama tends toward melodrama, but some players like it. Opus 44, No. 2, in E Minor has a first movement reminiscent of the opening of Mozart's 40th symphony, and it is the best of the opus. Opus 44, No. 3, is in E♭, and Op. 80 in F Minor. Opus 81 is a publisher's pastiche, where four individual movements were assembled into a quartet. Mendelssohn seems to have developed a mold for quartet writing, and all his quartets fit it. An evening devoted only to Haydn or to Mozart or Beethoven or Schumann would be enjoyable; one devoted to Mendelssohn would be tiresome. Some may like his two 2-viola quintets better than the quartets.

Robert Schumann (1810–1856)

Schumann held Mendelssohn in high esteem, but it seems the consensus of music historians that Schumann had far greater genius than his friend. Schumann was an intellectual who suffered from the biochemical anomaly we recognize today as a psychosis, and he died in an asylum for the insane after trying to drown himself in the Rhine. (Some forensic historians hold that he, Mozart and Schubert all died from consequences of syphilis, which Schumann acquired at birth while the others earned theirs.) He damaged one hand in a manner still disputed, and this barred a career as a pianist. He won recognition as a composer for the piano and editor of an influential music journal. Clara Wieck, the daughter of his music teacher, became his wife, became renowned as a pianist and outlived him by decades. In 1842, Schumann wrote the three string quartets of Op. 41. These are beautiful and rewarding for all of the players. The adagio of the third quartet contains a gorgeous dialogue between first violin and viola, a high point of music for the violist in the quartet literature.

Giuseppe Verdi (1813–1901)

Verdi is known for his many wonderful operas, most of which are performed all over the world. His one string quartet is no mere curiosity. It is a fine piece of quartet writing, written when he was 60. Considering that Verdi grew deservedly rich and famous from his wonderful operas, it shows almost fanaticism to remark, "What a pity Verdi wasted his time on all those operas when he could have been writing string quartets." (This could be said more justifiably of Schubert and other composers of unsuccessful operas.)

César Franck (1822–1890)

Franck was born in Liège in Belgium but pursued his career as organist and teacher in France. His sonata in A for violin and piano has remained very popular, and it is sometimes heard in versions for viola or cello. He wrote one string quartet, which is less popular than his piano quintet. His Symphony in D Minor enjoyed enormous popularity for a time, and his orchestral pieces are heard often.

Bedřich Smetana (1824–1884)

Like Beethoven, Smetana suffered from deafness in his later years. The son of a master brewer, he was a prodigy who played first violin in a Haydn quartet for his father's 51st birthday when he was only four. (He was the son of his father's third wife, the first two having died.) Two years later, he made his debut as a pianist. Bohemia was a province of the Austrian Empire during his lifetime, and Bedřich (Friedrich in German, the common language of the empire) was later acknowledged as the father of Czech music. The spread of nationalist movements across Europe during his lifetime led to a great interest in establishing

Slavic and, specifically, Czech music in his province, and Smetana became the leader. He wrote many operas, and he was director of the opera in Prague. Like Schumann, he died in an insane asylum. He is best known in the United States for the symphonic poem, *Vltava* (The Moldau) and the overture to his opera, *The Bartered Bride;* however, his first string quartet is a staple of the repertory, and his wonderful piano trio is heard occasionally.

This Bohemian composer wrote two string quartets, in E Minor and D Minor. Both are said to have programs depicting the composer's life. (Most string quartets are "absolute music," but a few have been given programs by their composers.) A loose translation of the program for the first is: I. the love of art in his youth, the unfulfilled inchoate yearnings, as well as forebodings of approaching troubles; II. a "quasi Polka" takes an example from his happy youth of his enthusiasm for this dance and uses its rhythms; III. the happiness of first love for the girl who later became his wife, and IV. the recognition of national music, the joy in its success; suddenly, the ringing in his ears, signified by a sustained high E on the violin, which presaged his deafness, and a painful remembrance of the joys and sorrows of his life, a faint ray of hope, and finally resignation to the inevitable fate. Whether or not the players think of the program that comes with it, this is a splendid quartet. It begins with an extended viola solo, and that instrument, along with the others, has much to do throughout the work. The beautiful F Minor *Largo sostenuto* is announced with a cadenza for cello solo.

Johannes Brahms (1833–1897)

Brahms was a north German, who settled in Vienna when he was 30. As a youth, he earned his living as a pianist in the saloons and brothels of the Hamburg waterfront. He was a pianist, who toured as accompanist for the Hungarian violinist Reményi, and his connections with him and Joachim brought him introductions to Liszt and to Schumann. He was hailed by Robert Schumann in an article of extravagant praise as the successor to Beethoven.

Brahms wrote much more than he allowed to be published. He left three string quartets, two string quintets and two string sextets along with a clarinet quintet as his chamber music without piano. The two quartets of Op. 51 and the single quartet of Op. 67 demand good players and experience. There are many tricky passages with two beats against three. An amateur quartet that can read through a Brahms quartet, however imperfectly, is no longer at beginner level. All of the players must be able to handle their instruments well and be reasonably secure in rhythm.

Alexander Borodin (1834–1901)

A Russian composer who had careers as a chemist and physician, Borodin styled himself a Sunday composer. (A career in science and an intense interest in music is not at all uncommon among us amateur chamber music players.) Borodin's two string quartets caused a sensation when they were performed in Paris, and they are said to have been the direct inspiration for the quartets of Debussy and Ravel. The first quartet, in A, is sometimes condemned for using a theme closely similar to one in Beethoven's Op. 130. In Borodin's hands, it sounds quite different, and we do not understand why it should be dismissed on that account. The second quartet, in D, contains melodies which were used in the musical comedy *Kismet*. The Nocturne movement is sometimes heard by itself in a string orchestra version. Both quartets are enjoyable for the players, being challenging in places but not too difficult. (Judgments of relative difficulty are mutable. What is incomprehensible for beginning players may become lucid when reexamined after more experience is obtained.)

Peter Ilyich Tchaikovsky (1834–1888)

Tchaikovsky is not thought of as a chamber music composer, but his work for strings include three quartets and a sextet, the *Souvenir de Florence,* as well as a piano trio dedicated to the memory of Nicholas Rubinstein, Anton's brother. The *Andante Cantabile* of the first quartet, Op. 11, is another movement often played by string orchestra.

Opus 22 is in F, and it has a rhapsodic first movement. The Op. 30 is in the difficult key of E♭ Minor, but it is worth the effort it requires. The quartets all are worthwhile, but they are heard infrequently. Tchaikovsky lived in fear that his homosexuality would be discovered, and he ended a suicide when he learned his secret would be divulged to the Czar.

Antonin Dvořák (1841–1904)

Dvořák was a Bohemian composer. He first achieved recognition when he was identified by a committee headed by Brahms searching out talent in the Austrian empire, of which Bohemia was a province until 1918. For a time, Dvořák played viola in the Prague Opera orchestra, of which Smetana was the director. His Slavonic Dances achieved great popularity and launched his career. He was much honored in his lifetime. His chamber music includes 14 string quartets, but not all of them are available at this writing. The opus numbers and numbering of the International Music Publishers series are misleading. They number the quartets 3 through 8.

Dvořák was one of the great composers of the 19th century and many of his works are standards of the symphonic and chamber music literature. Opus 96, "The American" quartet, is the best known. This was written along with Op. 97, a string quintet, during a summer Dvořák spent among his countrymen in northeastern Iowa at Spillville. He had been invited to the United States to become director of the institution which was the predecessor of the Juilliard School, and he spent two years in this country. The quartets are enjoyable for all of the players, and Op. 96 and Op. 51 are favorites. The Op. 34 contains a movement called "à la Polka," but the mood is different than the polka in the Smetana quartet. All of those available are worthwhile exploring, although the first violin would be well advised to study his part and put in fingerings beforehand. The International Edition quartets were edited by members of the Paganini Quartet, formed by Henri Temianka in the United States and which existed for 20 years after World War II. The Op. 9 quartet was completed by Günter Raphael in 1929. Its slow movement is the theme used in Dvořák's Romance for Violin and Orchestra. There is a project afoot to edit and revive Dvořák's early quartets. Judging from Op. 9, one should respect the composer's judgment in abandoning them.

Leoš Janáček (1854–1928)

Janáček wrote two programmatic quartets called *Intimate Letters* and *Kreutzer Sonata* (from the Tolstoy story). These are on our list of quartets to see if we can handle them. We have heard them and like them, but we have not seen the music.

Jean Sibelius (1865–1957)

Sibelius was a great Finnish composer, whose D Minor violin concerto, symphonies and other orchestral compositions are standard repertory. So is his one string quartet, appropriately called, *Intimate Voices*. Very little of his work was composed after his 60th year.

Arnold Schoenberg (1874–1951)

Schoenberg had an immense influence on the course of 20th century music. His sextet, *Transfigured Night*, written in his youth before his development of the tone row, is a stunning and lush romantic work which amateurs can appreciate. On the rare occasions when his later compositions are played, we amateurs listen respectfully and, so far, with no pleasure. We try.

Charles Ives (1874–1954)

Ives came into fashion after his death. His two quartets are beginning to be heard. He was among the most original and idiomatic of American composers.

Edward Elgar (1857–1934)

A fine string quartet in E Minor is among a few other chamber music compositions of Elgar. Best known for *Pomp and Circumstance*, the *Enigma Variations* and other orchestral works and the salon piece, *Salut d'Amour*, he is appreciated most in his native United Kingdom. Elgar's works are warm, romantic and expressive.

Ernest Bloch (1880–1959)

Bloch was a Swiss who immigrated to the United States. He had been a student of Ysäye before he became a composer. He published three quartets. He is best known for his rhapsody for cello and orchestra, *Schelomo*, and other works with a Jewish cast. His *Concerto Grosso* for orchestra is another fine work. He wrote very effective pieces for violin or viola and piano.

Béla Bartók (1881–1945)

Bartók was born in Hungary and died in New York. His six quartets are available and highly regarded. The ITSQ will have to work up to these. He was one of many composers whose genius was not appreciated until after his death.

Zoltán Kodály (1882–1967)

Kodály was another great Hungarian composer who, like Bartók, searched for folk music. His Op. 2 was one of his two string quartets.

Sergei Prokofiev (1891–1953)

A major Russian composer, Prokofiev spent much time in the West before returning to Russia at the height of Stalin's repression. He provided two string quartets. His music has been characterized as sardonic, witty, and sometimes percussive, but it is also very lyrical. His *Overture on Hebrew Themes,* for clarinet, piano and string quartet is something we worked on, but we never could assemble the required forces to try it.

Dmitry Shostakovich (1906–1975)

Shostakovich was a major composer of this century. In addition to other forms, he enriched chamber music with 15 string quartets.

Samuel Barber (1910–1981)

Barber wrote two movement quartet, the *Adagio* of which is heard most often in the version for string orchestra.

Some Other Composers

Alberto Ginestera (1916–1983) was a major Argentine composer who produced two conventional string quartets and one with soprano. The second is very enjoyable. Paul Hindemith (1895–1963) was a violist and composer. Aside from his *Achte Stücke für Streichquartett* of which we were thankful there were not "neun," the only one of his six quartets we have tried is the *Minimax,* which he wrote for his own quartet for fun. Hindemith has not come back into vogue yet.

Every once in a while, we hear quartets at concerts we find attractive. One of these was the first of five by Walter Piston (1894–1976), an American. The same could be said for the British composer, Benjamin Britten (1913–1976), who wrote several string quartets among many other works. Heitor Villa-Lobos (1887–1959) was a great and original Brazilian composer who wrote 17 string quartets, none of which we have ever heard. Darius Milhaud (1892–1974) was a French composer from an old Jewish family in Provence. He spent many years in the United States and was a prolific composer. Over a period of 50 years, he wrote 18 string quartets. George Rochberg (1918–) is an American who has written three quartets, the second with soprano.

Looking through the catalogue of a university library, we find quartets by Benjamin Lees (1924–), Ignaz von Beecke (1773–1803), William Laurence Bergsma (1921–), Franz Berwald (1796–1868; he was a Swedish composer), Boris Blacher (1903–1975), Frank Bridge (1879–1941), Elliott Carter (1908–), Alfredo Casella (1883–1947), Aaron Copland (1900–), Lukas Foss (1922–), Ernest Goldner (Gold) (1921–), Josef Matthias Hauer (1883–1959), Vagn Holboe (1909–), Karel Husa (1921–), Fritz Kreisler (1875–1962, the great violinist), Normand Lockwood (1906–), Charles Martin Loeffler (1861–1935), Jerome Momigny (1762–1838), Hans Pfitzner (1869–1949), Aloïs Reiser (1887–?), Albert Roussel (1869–1937), Arthur Sheppard (1880–1958), Seymour Shifrin (1926–), John Cage (1912–), Henry Cowell (1897–1965), Alan Hovhaness (1911–), Virgil Thomson (1896–) and William Walton (1902–1983). For the fact that I do not know any of these works, I can only offer the explanation given by Samuel Johnson to a woman rating him for errors in his dictionary: "Ignorance. Sheer ignorance."

XII. Notes on the Literature

Verbal description provides only opinion and no more gives the reader an idea of what the music is like than a description of the taste of wine lets a reader savor it. Nevertheless, if the characteristics of an unknown vintage are compared with one we know, we may be encouraged to try it. Absolute judgments of difficulty are personal and mutable, but one can compare works and highlight difficult passages. The reader should remember the author's caveat: as a quartet player he is a pretty good pharmaceutical scientist. (Being an ethical and forthright man, at least when it comes to fiddle playing, I describe my attainments as a quartet player as objectively as possible. Usually, I say something like, "After many years of hard work, I have achieved mediocrity." People who have never heard me play assume modesty. Invariably, *never having heard me,* they describe me to others as an "accomplished" or "fine" violinist. This provides yet another reason for discouraging audiences for amateur string quartets. Why destroy illusions?) The reader may decide for himself whether undertaking to paint word pictures of the standard literature is foolhardy or courageous.

Juan Crisóstomo de Arriaga

The three quartets were published in Paris in 1824, and they are available in an International edition at reasonable price. Hence, they are played.

No. 1 in D Minor—*Allegro, Adagio con espressione, Minuetto/Trio,* an eight-measure *Adagio,* and *Allegretto.* This is very pretty music, with a Spanish flavor. All the players get melodies. The viola gets the melody in treble clef in the concluding major section of the first movement. He should be advised to stay in position throughout. The *Adagio* begins with a held half-note, and this always caused problems in the count. An effective solution we found was for the first fiddle to announce that this will be held three beats.

No. 2 in A — *Allegro con brio, Andante* (theme, five variations and a coda in D), *Minuetto (Scherzo)* in A / Trio in D Minor, *Andante ma non troppo* in ¾ alternating with a cut time *Allegro*. There are few traps for reasonably good players. The viola has the solo in D Minor in Variation 3, written in treble clef, but this holds no problems. The second fiddle shows his worth in the fifth variation, having as virtuosic a part as the first.

No. 3 in E♭ — *Allegro, Pastorale (Andantino)* in G, *Minuetto* (C Minor), *Trio* (C), *Presto agitato*. The Pastorale was difficult to count for us. OK, me. This *Andantino* is slower than *Andante*.

Ludwig van Beethoven —
The Early Quartets, Op. 18, Nos. 1-6

Much searching analysis has been expended on the Beethoven string quartets. Even more nonsense has been written about them. This second observation lessens my inhibitions. This set of six was published in 1801, two years before Haydn's unfinished Op. 103.

No. 1 in F — *Allegro con brio, Adagio affetuoso ed appassionato* (D Minor), *Scherzo (Allegro Molto) / Trio, Allegro*. The high point is the slow movement, a beautiful melody for first fiddle. The quartet is a favorite in the set.

No. 2 in G — *Allegro, Adagio cantabile* (C), *Scherzo allegro / Trio* (C), *Allegro molto quasi presto*. There are no great problems here. Everyone stays busy.

No. 3 in D — *Allegro, Andante con moto* (B♭), *Allegro* (major, minor, major), *Presto*. The second fiddle begins the melody in the slow movement in the G string and should be alert to be assertive on the swell. The concluding Presto, in 6/8, is universally called the "Mexican Hat Dance" from the relentless character of the theme. Everyone gets exercise.

No. 4 in C Minor — *Allegro ma non tanto, Scherzo (Andante*

scherzoso quasi Allegretto), Minuetto/Trio (four flats), *Allegro.* Some
of Beethoven's best works were in C Minor. His Op. 1, No. 3, piano
trio, his Op. 9, No. 3, string trio and his fifth symphony are examples.
Haydn, much more prolific, wrote only one quartet in this key, Op. 17,
No. 4. (Consider this a contribution from the Office of Unimportant
Information.) Somehow, we find ourselves playing No. 4 more often
than others in the set. This is a magnificent quartet. The problems
come in the last movement. The four players roll comfortably along until they come to a section in C major, which often throws the first fiddle
off rhythm. Back to the minor, and the first fiddle feels good about
handling sextuplet arpeggios, then he feels panic when confronted
with a concluding *Prestissimo.* He is already playing as fast as he is able.
Prestissimo means play faster than he can. The vacuum cleaner recep-
tacle can hold the dropped notes the next morning.

    No. 5 in A—*Allegro, Minuetto/Trio, Andante cantabile* (in D
with five variations), *Allegro.* Beethoven admired greatly the Mozart
K464. This quartet was written on the same plan. Of course, Beethoven
wrote like himself, and Mozart was Mozart. If I had to choose, I like
the Mozart better, but I do not have to choose. I can play both. I am
not aware that anyone has compared these two quartets with the Haydn
Op. 55, No. 1, which is in the same key and was written after the
Mozart, which was among the six Mozart dedicated to him. This has
similarities in form, especially in the interlude of whole note chords in
the last movement. We will leave this conjecture for some drudge in
a graduate school. (It should be worth at least an MFA.) The quartet
needs a good first fiddle throughout, and it seems a little top heavy in
first violin.

    No. 6 in B♭—*Allegro con brio, Adagio ma non troppo (E♭),
Scherzo (Allegro)/Trio, La Malinconia,* and *Adagio,* followed by
Allegretto quasi Allegro, returning to *Adagio,* then *Allegretto,* and
finishing with a rousing *Prestissimo.* This last movement has the instruction, "Questo pezzo si deve trattare colla più gran delicatezza"
(play this movement with greatest delicacy). Beethoven took great
pride in his grasp of Italian, and he delighted in long qualifying
phrases. Carping critics have castigated his use of the language;
however, the Office of Unimportant Information points out that he
antedated the standardization of the Italian language by Mazzini in the

Risorgimento. Beethoven seems to have been trying to say something novel in this quartet, but we have not figured out what it is yet. The last movement, with all its changes in rhythm and mood, is very difficult to hold together.

Beethoven — Middle Period Quartets, Op. 59, Op. 74, Op. 95

The three of Op. 59 were published in 1806. By this time, Beethoven was solidly in favor with Prince Lichnowsky, Count Rasoumovsky and the other music-loving nobility. Andreas Rasoumovsky was the Russian ambassador to the Habsburg Empire. The Op. 59 quartets were dedicated to him, and they contain Russian themes. The quartets often are referred to as "Beethoven's Rasoumovsky Quartets." The aristocracy of the capital provided him with an annuity, which made him financially stable until the financial panic accompanying the Napoleonic wars made him dependent on his own cupidity in dealing and double-dealing with publishers. (Unlike Haydn, Beethoven was not the kind of man one wants to use as a role model for his children, unless they, too, were geniuses.) More important from our standpoint, they provided him with professional string quartet players as a laboratory. This was the beginning of the professional string quartet, and it spelled the end of the era when composers had to keep in mind the technical limitations of us amateur players. We read with satisfaction that the professionals complained to Beethoven about the technical difficulties he provided them — and with exasperation at his refusing to compromise with them. He left us with no choice but to work out the technical problems.

Op. 59, No. 1 in F (the "first Rasoumovsky") — *Allegro, Allegretto vivace e sempre scherzando* (B♭), *Adagio molto e mesto* (F Minor), *Theme russe (Allegro).* This is a magnificent work, beginning with a long sweeping cello solo which is taken over by the first violin. Everybody works, and there are beautiful duets for the violins and viola/cello. The "mesto" direction in the *Adagio* means "sad." It does not nearly describe the mood of the first violin who has to try to play six measures of 64th notes, studded with accidentals, in a four-flat key at the end of the movement. What is the Italian for "desperation?" Trying to sight-read this has proved impossible, and practice has not made perfect. Hope springs eternal. Maybe we'll be able to leap this chasm some evening.

Op. 59, No. 2, in E Minor (the "second Rasoumovsky") — *Allegro, Molto Adagio* in E "Si tratta questo pezzo con molto di sentimento," *Allegretto* (major section is the Russian theme), *Finale (Presto).* The *Adagio* is one of the most gripping experiences in quartet literature. The quartet is very difficult, but it is worth the effort. Once in my lifetime, I played the first violin part well. I tried many times before and more since, but the once is a shining memory.

Op. 59, No. 3, in C (the "third Rasoumovsky") — *Introduzione (Andante con moto)/Allegro vivace, Andante con moto quasi Allegretto, Minuetto/Trio* (in F), *Allegro molto.* Do not be misled by the key signature into thinking this is easy. Beethoven conceded nothing to the players. The last movement is fugal, beginning with a 10 measure exposition by the solo viola. The next 10 measures are a second violin–viola duet, then follows another 10 measures as a trio with added cello until the first violin enters. A violist who feels animosity toward the first fiddle has the perfect opportunity to break him in this movement by setting the tempo very fast. Seeing the first struggling to play in tune and in time, with his left hand high on the E string is comical, unless one faces a mirror. The movement requires great stamina from all the players. The slow movement is beautifully constructed, with cello pizzicato.

Op. 74 in E♭ ("The Harp") — *Poco Adagio/Allegro, Adagio ma non troppo* (A♭), *Presto, Allegretto con variationi.* This quartet was composed in 1809. Its nickname comes from the abundance of arpeggios and pizzicato passages. The first violin would be advised to study his part well before reading it in a quartet session. Among other delights are 25 measures of bowed arpeggios, which begin against a *pizzicato* accompaniment of the lower strings. The lovely slow movement, with great interest for all players, has rapid staccato passage work for the second violin and pizzicato for the viola. The *Presto* has an interlude in C, *Più presto quasi prestissimo* where Beethoven directs the players to imagine the 3/4 beat as a 6/8 beat (two measures as one). This has not been a problem. The last movement accelerates to *Allegro* near the end. Because everyone has 16th note passages, the temptation to make this a *Presto* is diminished.

Op. 95 in F Minor ("Serioso") — The quartet was composed in 1810, and its sobriquet derives from a descriptor for the third movement. The order is *Allegro con brio, Allegretto ma non troppo* (in D), *Allegro assai vivace ma serioso* (F Minor/D/C Minor/F Minor), *Larghetto espressivo/Allegretto agitato/Allegro* (F) in cut time. It is a rouser at the finish.

Beethoven — Late Period Quartets, Op. 127, Op. 130–133, Op. 135

Beethoven's final quartets were written during the last three years of his life. He was completely deaf by this time. He was a famous man, and he needed to pay no attention to conventions like having four movements and the rules for progression of keys that constrained his predecessors. Beethoven had reached the pinnacle where he was the final authority. Music critics of his time had hard choices to make. The worst judgment they were willing to make was that passages of great beauty were mixed with evidence of premature senility. Beethoven was in his mid fifties and ill.

He had long since ignored the technical limitations of players and overridden their objections to difficulties. For Beethoven, it was pure music of the intellect, for he could not hear it save in his mind. Of all that has been written about Beethoven, perhaps these quartets are considered his highest achievement. For the amateur quartet player, one of the best ways to appreciate these monumental works is to listen with score in hand. If relations between the quartet members can stand the stress, try to read through them after practice.

Op. 127 in E♭ — *Maestoso/Allegro/Maestoso/Allegro, Adagio, ma non troppo e molto cantabile/Andante con moto/Adagio molto expressivo, Scherzando vivace/Allegro/Presto, Finale/Allegro con moto*. This quartet begins and ends in E♭. Between the first passage and the last, one is sure to find his favorite key signature. Of course, the music modulates to all of the more difficult keys. Prince Nicholas Galitzin, who commissioned three of the last quartets — Op. 127,

Op. 130, and Op. 132 were dedicated to him — complained that it required long and careful study to get the music out. The first movement is deceptive. Not easy, it can be handled by reasonably competent players. The slow movement has a wonderful rising figuration traded between the first violin and cello in the reprise of the first *Adagio* section after the second, cut time *Adagio*. The first *Adagio* begins in 12/8 and goes to the *Andante* in 4/4. The *Andante* is difficult to count. Maybe if this were counted in 16ths...

Op. 130 in B♭ — The ITSQ got through this after many failed efforts! The six movements are *Adagio ma non troppo/Allegro, Presto/L'Istesso tempo, Andante con moto ma non troppo (Poco scherzoso)* [with all this help from the composer — *Andante* with movement but not too much, somewhat like a scherzo — one should have no trouble with tempo and style. I am fuddled; I listen to a professional quartet play it and try vainly to imitate them. Its key signature of B♭ Minor (five flats) does not make it easier], *Alla danza tedesca (Allegro assai), Cavatina (Adagio molto espressivo), Finale (Allegro).* The alternation of tempi in the first movement can be handled by considering the *Allegro* double the speed of the *Adagio*, but one has to be equally alert for key changes. The cut time *Presto* (in B♭ Minor) is followed by the *L'Istesso tempo,* 6/4, in the major. This is played as if it were 2/4 with triplet pairs in each measure. It is fun. The German dance frolics along. It is a great exercise in violin technique.

The *Cavatina* is a beautiful song. At one point, the composer directed "beklemmt," which might be translated as "anxious." This is an outstandingly beautiful movement, masterful in its simplicity. It can be played by a first violin with a broken E string! There are no excursions past a third-position A♭ on the A string. Most of Beethoven's music for violin makes this fiddler claw high on the fingerboard. (One may speculate that the composer heard high-frequency tones better than low notes. By the time he wrote this movement, he heard no external sounds.) To our knowledge, no musicologists have commented on this point. The Office of Unimportant Information considers this an outstandingly trivial contribution to Beethoven musicology. The *Finale* is a dazzling, joyous 2/4 romp. It is the last chamber music Beethoven wrote. It was a substitute for the *Grosse Fuge* (great fugue), the original last movement. The fugue was published separately as Op. 133.

Professional quartets sometimes play Op. 130 in the original version, with the fugue as finale, a testimony both to their devotion to authenticity and their physical stamina.

Op. 131 in C♯ Minor — *Adagio, ma non troppo e molto cantabile, Allegro molto vivace Allegro moderato* (11 measures), *Andante, ma non troppo e molto espressivo, Presto, Adagio quasi un poco andante* (28 measures), *Allegro.* The first movement of the seven is the most notable. It begins fugally with what must have been perceived as strange harmonies. The notorious Schnittke cadenza for Beethoven's violin concerto does not seem like such a violation of Beethoven's style when it is compared with what Beethoven himself produced here.

Op. 132 in A Minor — *Assai sostenuto / Allegro, Allegro ma non tanto, Molto adagio, Heiliger Dankgesang eines Genesen an die Gottheit, in der lydischen Tonart* (prayerful song to the Deity for his recovery in the Lydian mode). *Andante / Molto adagio, Alla Marcia, assai vivace / Presto, Allegro appassionato* — This preceded the Op. 130 and Op. 131 in composition date, but it was assigned a later opus number by the publisher. The last movement is a pre–Strauss waltz in everything but name.

Op. 133 in B♭ (Grosse Fuge) This is sometimes heard in a version for string orchestra. It was published after Beethoven's death. It is thrilling!

Op. 135 in F (published posthumously) — *Allegretto, Vivace, Lento assai, Andante e tranquillo (G♭?),* "Muss es sein? Es muss sein! Es muss sein!" *Grave, ma non troppo tratto / Allegro* — Beethoven had written the question, "must it be?" and the answer. This, the last complete quartet, is less demanding than the previous quartets of the group.

Alexander Borodin

Quartet No. 1 in A — *Moderato / Allegro, Andante con moto, Scherzo (Prestissimo) / Trio / Prestissimo, Andante / Allegro risoluto.* The *Trio* has fingered harmonics, which lie well and are not difficult. This quartet has been denigrated because a first movement theme is identical with a secondary theme from the last movement of Beethoven's

Op. 130. It seems a ridiculous complaint. The quartet is worthwhile buying and playing, although it is not nearly as lush as the second quartet. If this had been Borodin's only quartet, we suspect it would be respected more than it is.

Quartet No. 2 in D—*Allegro moderato/Animato, Scherzo (Allegro), Nocturne (Andante), Finale (Andante/Vivace).* Many of the melodies in this quartet will be recognizable from their use in a musical comedy. The *Nocturne* is heard often in a string orchestra version. This has some marvelous "echoing dialogue passages" between the first violin and cello and the first violin and second. It is a favorite quartet for determining if one's companions have any romance in their souls.

Johannes Brahms

Op. 51, No. 1, in C Minor—*Allegro, Romanze (Poco adagio), Allegretto molto moderato e commodo (F Minor)/Un poco più animated (F Major), Finale (Allegro).* Getting to the level to play the Brahms quartets was a major achievement for our group. We worked on the first a long time. In retrospect, the quartets do not seem at all difficult. A couple of problems we had were the 3/2 time signature in the first movement and broken triplets in the lovely F Minor *Romanze.* The quartets have gratifying parts for all the players.

Op. 51, No. 2 in A Minor—*Allegro non troppo, Andante moderato, Quasi minuetto, Moderato/Allegretto, Tempo di minuetto, Finale (Allegro non assai).* Once past No. 1 the second presented no problems. There is a lot of A Major in the quartet, a key we like playing. We love the variations for first fiddle in the first movement...

Op. 67 in B♭—*Vivace, Andante, Agitato (Allegretto non troppo)/Trio, Coda, Poco allegretto con variazioni/Doppio Movimento*—In a first reading of the Op. 67 quartet first movement, which begins in 6/8 and has passages in 2/4, the second violin asked to gather forces at one place where a change occurs. After several minutes of universal confusion, it was discovered that the second fiddle part changes at a different place than the others. The practical solution to mastering this movement lay in the realization that all of it should be counted 2/4, the 6/8 being played as if it were triplet pairs. The third movement uses the viola singing out the melody, in D Minor, un-muted with accompaniment of *con sordino* violins and cello. The viola gets two chances. After the *Trio,* where the (still) muted first violin and the viola have a dialogue, it is back to the top, then a Coda in D Major. This movement provides incentive for violists to study this quartet and violinists to study viola. It is an inspiration in effective use of the tone color of the viola. The viola also gets some gratifying passages in the last movement.

Claude Debussy

Debussy wrote but one string quartet, a staple of the literature. It is usually found paired with the Ravel Quartet. [It requires players with experience, but it is not difficult to get through in recordings.]

Op. 10 in G Minor—*Animé et très décidé, Assez vif et bien rythmé, Andantino, doucement expressif, Très modéré.*

Antonin Dvořák

Following is a listing of the Dvořák quartets where "B" denotes the chronological numbers assigned by Dr. Jarmil Burghauser in his thematic catalog of Dvořák's work and S is the Ottokar Šourek catalog number.

Date	Opus	Key	B	S	Int.
1873	9	F Minor	37	20	—
1874	16	A Minor	45	25	1
1876	80	E	57	35	5
1877	34	D Minor	75	52	2
1878–9	51	E♭	92	62	3
1881	61	C	121	82	4
1893	96	F	179	118	6
1895	106	G	192	128	8
1895	105	A♭	193	127	7

Op. 9 in F Minor, B37, S20 — *Moderato/Allegro con brio, Andante con moto quasi Allegretto, Tempo di Valse/Allegretto, Allegro molto.* Dvořák apparently abandoned this early quartet. The edition available was completed and edited by Günter Raphael. The second movement should seem familiar. The theme was used later in a *Romance for Violin and Orchestra.* Basing the conclusion on limited experience, one should credit Dvořák with knowing what he was doing in giving up on this one.

Op. 34 in D Minor, B75, S52 — *Allegro, Allegretto scherzando/Trio (2/4)/3/8, quasi l'istesso tempo, Adagio (con sordino), Finale (Poco Allegro).* This sounds like authentic Dvořák, melodic, rhythmic and interesting to the players. The only edition we found available is hard to read in the places where the first violin plays leger notes high above the staff. Presumably to save paper costs, the publisher compressed these. Where there is choice, it is worth spending more money to get a spaciously-planned edition of any quartet part.

Op. 51 in E♭, B92, S62 — *Allegro ma non troppo, Dumka [Elegie] (Andante con moto/Vivace/Andante con moto/Presto, Romanze (Andante con moto), Finale.* This is a marvelous piece of music. It was commissioned by the Florentine Quartet, who asked that it be in the composer's Slavonic idiom. The Dumka movement begins with a wonderful dialogue between the first violin and the viola. It takes some ensemble practice to master the changes in tempo in this movement. The *Romanze* is well-named. It is gorgeous.

Op. 80 in E, B57, S35 — *Allegro, Andante con moto, Allegro scherzando/Trio, Allegro con brio.* This needs practice of parts beforehand. There are many excursions to high registers for the first violin. The slow movement is a lovely song in E Minor. Despite its opus number, this is an early quartet, and it shows less Slavonic character than the later quartets.

Op. 61 in C, B121, S82 — *Allegro, Poco Adagio et molto cantabile Allegro vivo/Trio, Finale (Vivace).* The first and last movements have some very high notes for the first violin. He would be well advised to locate the notes and finger his part before trying to read this with the other quartet members. The slow movement presents a counting problem. The time signature is given as 4/4(12/8), and there is much 3 against 2. Everyone should study all the parts. It is useful to change count when the occasion demands.

Op. 96 in F (The "American"), B179, S118—*Allegro ma non troppo, Lento (6/8), Molto vivace Finale (Vivace ma non troppo)*. This quartet is a joy for all the players. The violist begins the melody in the first movement and has a prominent part throughout, except for the second movement, where everyone but the violist has melodic passages. Nevertheless, the accompaniment figures played by the viola here are very interesting. One of the International edition quartets, this contains much of what Donald Cohen, a California amateur, calls "false treble" in the cello part. Cohen defines false treble as music written in the treble clef but intended to sound an octave lower. This causes great difficulty for amateur cellists, especially in sight-reading. (We have heard of a convention that treble clef following bass clef should be sounded an octave lower than written, while treble clef following tenor clef sounds as written. The editor of the cello part appears to have followed this convention.) Cohen offered corrected parts, at cost, in bass and tenor clefs through ACMP. These "Cello Conversion Kits" could be cemented over the "false treble" passages. This true philanthropy has left countless amateur string quartets in his debt. We recently discovered that like conversions can be accomplished by several computer programs.

Op. 105 in A flat, B193, S127—*Adagio ma non troppo/Allegro appassionato, Molto vivace, Lento molto cantabile (F Major), Allegro non tanto*. It is dismaying to open this quartet to an Adagio in seven flats (A♭ Minor), but the passage is relatively short, and it works out well. A reward is that the *Lento* movement is in F. We have become increasing fond of this quartet with repeated playing and listening. It is not as difficult as Op. 61 or Op. 80.

Op. 106 in G, B192, S128—*Allegro moderato, Adagio ma non troppo, Molto vivace, Finale (Andante sostenuto/Allegro con fuoco)*. The *Adagio* is outstanding in its beauty.

Edward Elgar (1857–1934)

Quartet in E Minor, Op. 83—*Allegro moderato, Piacevole (Poco Andante), Allegro molto*. This quartet is well worth obtaining. It begins with a 12/8 movement which looks as though it might give a rhythm problem—but it does not. The second movement begins with an extended song played by the second violin.

César Franck

Quartet in D—*Poco Lento/Allegro, Scherzo, Larghetto (5♯), Finale (Allegro molto/Larghetto/Allegro molto/Vivace)*. The many changes in key and tempo make this difficult to sight-read for a quartet. Both violins have excursions into high altitudes. Our experience has been limited. It went well one time and in fits and starts another.

Edvard Grieg

Op. 27 in G Minor—*Un poco andante/Allegro molto ed agitato, Romanze (andantino/allegro agitato), Allegro molto marcato, Finale (Lento/Presto al Saltarello)*. This is a real rouser. It does not seem much like chamber music, but it is wonderful physical exercise. This is the first of three Grieg quartets and the only one easily available.

Franz Josef Haydn

The published editions of Haydn's string quartets include 83, of which the six of Op. 3 are of dubious authenticity—now thought to have been written by a monk named Romanus Hofstetter—and the seven of Op. 51 are an arrangement of another work, "The Seven Last Words of Christ."

The Peters edition of Haydn quartets was originally two cumbersome volumes, in which the works were arbitrarily ordered and consecutively numbered. This was superseded in 1918 by an edition of four volumes, of which the first two were the "Celebrated" quartets, again arbitrarily selected by the editors, Andreas Moser and Hugo Dechert. (Moser was a Hungarian violinist, born in 1859, who was precluded from a career by a nervous disorder. He became the assistant of Joseph Joachim in Berlin. Dechert was a cellist who was a member of Joachim's string quartet.)

In their foreword to the 1918 edition, Moser and Dechert stated that they had selected 30 among the most beautiful and representative of Haydn's quartets. One may disagree with the selection, but this is a matter of taste. The publishers committed an offense to reason and an egregious disservice to generations of quartet players by use of the adjective "Celebrated." Such is the authority of the written word that generations of string quartet players have assumed that the 30 quartets selected by Moser and Dechert are the very best of Haydn, and they ignore all the others.

The volumes are littered with two sets of arbitrary numbers assigned by the publisher, and only the first two have the opus numbers printed on the music. (Opus numbers are assigned by music publishers, and they do not necessarily have any relation to chronology of composition. Opus 168 of Schubert, for example, is an early work, while his Opus 29 is a late one. With Haydn, on the other hand, the opus numbers are related to order of composition, and they should be written in where they are omitted.)

In a recent book on chamber music, Berger omitted discussion of the other Haydn quartets on the basis that most people play only the famous ones. Many quartet players buy only these so-called "Celebrated" quartets and thereby miss a great number of magnificent works. If one accepts the judgment that all Haydn quartets from Op. 9 on are masterpieces, then the "Celebrated" volumes contain only 28 of 60 works, excluding Op. 51. Wechsberg stated that the quartets in the editions of the famous Haydn and Mozart are better than the other volumes. The statement is valid for Mozart but not Haydn. With Mozart, the 10 famous quartets begin with K387, the masterpieces of his maturity, while the others end with K173, juvenilia. Thus, the division of Mozart quartets into celebrated and ignored has justification. With Haydn, the division is arbitrary. It is fatuous to state that the three Haydn quartets of Op. 54, annointed by the publisher as renowned, are better or more appreciated than their contemporary three of Op. 55, relegated to Vol. III. Any amateur quartet library should make the acquisition of all of the published Haydn volumes a priority.

Haydn Op. 1 and Op. 2—These are generally five-movement works which antedate Haydn's development of the string quartet as we know it. They are well worth looking at, like early Mozart quartets. They are played little, both because the later quartets are more interesting and because none of them was included among the famous quartets by Moser and Dechert. Most have an *Adagio* at the center, flanked by minuets and with fast movements as first and last. Op. 1, No. 3, begins with an *Adagio* and has a *Presto* as third movement. Op. 1, No. 5, is a three-movement work with no minuets; it is thought to have been a symphony. Op. 2, No. 6, begins with an *Adagio* theme with four variations. Violin players may well enjoy playing through the first violin parts of all of these quartets as practice.

Op. 1, No. 1, in B♭—*Presto, Minuetto/Trio, Adagio/Minuetto/Trio, Presto.*

Op. 1, No. 2, in E♭.*Allegro molto/Minuetto/Trio, Adagio, Minuetto/Trio, Presto.*

Op. 1, No. 3, in D—*Adagio, Minuetto/Trio, Presto, Minuetto/Trio, Presto.*

Op. 1, No. 4, in G—*Presto, Minuetto/Trio, Adagio, Minuetto/Trio, Presto.*

Op. 1, No. 5, in B♭—*Allegro, Andante, Allegro assai.*

Op. 1, No. 6, in C—*Presto assai, Minuetto/Trio, Adagio, Minuetto/Trio, Presto.*

Op. 2, No. 1, in A—*Allegro, Minuetto/Trio, Poco Adagio, Minuetto/Trio, Allegro molto.*

Op. 2, No. 2, in E—*Allegro, Minuetto/Trio, Adagio, Minuetto/Trio, Presto.*

Op. 2, No. 3, in E♭—*Allegro molto, Minuetto/Trio, Adagio, Minuetto/Trio,* (with three variations), *Allegro.*

Op. 2, No. 4, in F—*Presto, Minuetto/Trio, Adagio non troppo, Minuetto/Trio, Allegro.*

Op. 2, No. 5, in D—*Presto, Minuetto/Trio, Largo cantabile, Alla breve, Minuetto/Trio, Presto.*

Op. 2, No. 6, in B♭—*Adagio* (four variations), *Minuetto/Trio, Presto, Minuetto/Trio, Presto.*

Op. 3, The "Hofstetter Quartets"—Some musicologists claim these were written by a monk, Romanus Hofstetter, who had Haydn's name substituted by a Paris publisher when the parts were being engraved. Thus, the famous Haydn Serenade, from Op .3, No. 5, may not be Haydn at all. This quartet and No. 3 were included in Vol. II of the "Celebrated Quartets," so they are played more than far worthier works. In spite of their dubious parentage, the two we have played seem like competent quartet writing.

Op. 3, No. 1, in E — *Allegro molto, Minuetto/trio, Andantino grazioso, Presto.*

Op. 3, No. 2, in C — *Fantasia con Variazioni* (four of them), *Minuetto/trio, Presto.*

Op. 3, No. 3, in G — **"Bagpipe"** — This gets its name from the minuet, where the first violin plays a melody over a sustained open D string drone.

Op. 3, No. 4, in B♭ — *Allegro moderato, Adagio/Presto.*

Op. 3, No. 5, in F ("With the Serenade") — The famous "Haydn Serenade," in C, is played by the muted first violin against a pizzicato accompaniment by the lower strings. Its inclusion in the celebrated volume assures it is played often. Many players obtained their introduction to quartet playing plucking the accompaniment.

Op. 3, No. 6, in A — *Presto, Adagio, Minuetto/Trio, Scherzando.*

Op. 9 and Op. 17 — These are the real thing. I infer that Haydn attempted to vary the same or similar thematic material through all four movements. Haydn was blessed with good violinists on his staff throughout his long career in charge of music for the Esterházy princes, so the first violin part in many of his quartets has some difficult passages with double-stops and high positions. Favorites include Op. 9, No. 6, in A and Op. 17, No. 4, in C Minor, his only quartet in that key, but all of them are worth spending time on. The amateur can develop his own favorites among them.

Op. 9, No. 1, in C — *Moderato, Minuetto/Trio, Adagio (F), Presto.*

Op. 9, No. 2, in E♭ — *Allegro moderato, Minuetto/trio, Adagio, Allegro molto.* This is one of the "Celebrated," but I would not have picked it.

Op. 9, No. 3, in G — *Allegro moderato, Minuetto/Trio, Largo, Presto.*

Op. 9, No. 4, in D Minor — *Allegro, moderato, Minuetto/Trio,*

Adagio cantabile, Presto. This would be a candidate along with the following two. Picking one would be arbitrary—of course. The first violin gets to play (easy) double stops in the *Trio,* thereby providing a temporary quintet.

Op. 9, No. 5, in B♭ —*Poco Adagio, Minuetto / Trio, Largo cantabile, Presto.* I like listening to and playing this. The cello has some beautiful figures in the opening movement, which has four variations.

Op. 9, No. 6, in A —*Presto, Minuetto / Trio, Adagio, Allegro.* It is fun fiddling in the first movement. The cut-time *Adagio,* in E, is very effective. The last movement is a very short exercise in scales even playing the repeats. One finishes the quartet marveling at what Haydn was able to accomplish with simple materials.

Op. 17, No. 1, in E —*Moderato, Minuetto / Trio, Adagio, Presto.* The second violin gets to show musicianship in the broken-sixths accompaniment passages in the E Major slow movement. We like this quartet.

Op. 17, No. 2, in F —*Moderato, Minuetto / Trio, Adagio, Allegro di molto.* They are all enjoyable in this set.

Op. 17, No. 3, in E♭ —*Andante grazioso, Minuetto / Trio, Adagio, Allegro molto.* The quartet begins with a theme and four variations. The first fiddle gets to show virtuosity.

Op. 17, No. 4, in C Minor —*Moderato, Minuetto / Trio, Adagio cantabile, Allegro.* Considering Haydn's versatility in key signatures, it is remarkable that this is the only C minor quartet.

Op. 17, No. 5, in G —*Moderato, Minuetto / Trio, Adagio, Presto.* This is the representative Op. 17 among the "Celebrated." It would not have been my choice.

Op. 17, No. 6, in D —*Presto, Minuetto / Trio, Largo, Presto.* Decide yourself.

The Op. 20 quartets: These were written in 1771. Each is individual in character, and the four movements within each of them although related by keys, are more individual than in the Op. 9 and Op. 17 quartets. Three of the quartets, nos. 1, 5 and 6, have fugues for finales, and two, No. 3 in G and No. 5 in F, are minor-key works. The last three were included in the "Celebrated" set, but the first three are just as worthwhile.

Op. 20, No. 1, in E♭—*Allegro moderato, Minuetto/Trio, Affettuoso e sostenuto, Presto.* The second violin has a solo in the seventh measure and viola and cello get solo passages in the first movement. The minuet in the same key features a cello solo in the *Trio.* The slow movement, 3/8, is in A♭, the subdominant. It is a remarkable movement. The only comparable slow movement is in Mozart's K428 quartet in the same key. It finishes with a syncopated 2/4 in the tonic, ending in a *pianissimo.*

Op. 20, No. 2, in C—*Moderato, Adagio, Minuetto/Trio, Allegro (Fugue with four subjects).* The quartet begins with a cello solo. There is much work here for the cellist in the tenor clef. The violist has a solo, and the second fiddle has much interesting material. The gorgeous *Adagio* is in C Minor, 4/4, and it begins with a unison of a dramatic theme, and has to be played slowly. The minuet in C has double-stopping for the first fiddle, and its trio has three flats, with a unison melody in the second section. It finishes with a four-subject fugue in 6/8 time, one of those movements where some players may find it useful to count in 2/4 and in 6/8 at different places. The Haydn quartet fugues are all directed to be played softly until close to the end, when a *forte* direction is given.

Op. 20, No. 3, in G Minor—*Allegro con spirito, Minuetto Allegretto, Poco Adagio, Allegro molto.* The first movement has great interest for all the players. The minuet is in G minor, with the *Trio* in E♭—I think. The slow movement, in G, has solo passages for the viola and cello. The finale is in 4/4, and it has many canonic passages. It is started by the second violin, and there are many canonic passages. In the Peters edition, the second violin part repeats are written out. I wrote a note on the first violin part, instructing the player to tell the others to play both repeats.

Op. 20, No. 4, in D—*Allegro di molto, Un poco adagio affetuoso, Minuetto (Allegretto alla zingarese)/Trio, Poco scherzando.* This and the following two probably are played more by amateurs than the preceding quartets in the set, simply because they were dubbed "celebrated." The first movement is most effective played fast, as directed, but most of my colleagues tend to relax the tempo. It still works. The slow movement, in the minor, is 2/4 and is best counted as 4/8. It is a theme with four variations. The second violin gets the star role in the first variation, and the cellist takes center stage for the second. The first violin is well advised to annotate the fingerings for his part for the third variation so he can stay in position instead of scrambling around the fingerboard. Dynamics have to be observed in the last variation. The cellist gets interesting figurations in the trio between the playings of the "Gypsy" minuet.

Op. 20, No. 5, in F Minor — *Allegro moderato, Minuetto/Trio, Adagio, Finale (Fugue with two subjects).* The first movement is one of the most dramatic in the quartet literature. It sounds more romantic than classical. The remainder of the quartet is interesting, but there is no way it can match the opening. The *Finale* is a fugue on a theme by Handel. Like all the Haydn fugues, it is to be played softly until the end.

Op. 20, No. 6, in A — *Allegro molto e scherzando, Adagio cantabile, Minuetto/Trio, Allegro (Fugue with three subjects).* I do not know why we play this less often than the others in the opus. It is a delight, especially for the first violin.

The Op. 33 Quartets — Haydn wrote these ten years after Op. 20, advertising them as having been written in a new and special way. They were the inspiration for the great quartets by Mozart. Numbers 2, 3 and 6 are included among the "Celebrated," while the others are relegated to Vol. IV. Hans Keller does not like No. 4 and he is an expert. I like it very much, which might lead the ungenerous to question my taste but not my courage.

Op. 33, No. 1, in B Minor — *Allegro moderato, Scherzando allegro/Trio, Andante, Presto.* The B minor *Scherzando* has some bariolage for the first violin on F♯. I eventually learned that this should be played in the second position, reaching back with the first fiinger on the E. The *Trio* is in the major, but the five sharps lie well. The theme of the D major *Andante* stays in the mind for days. The *Presto*, ending in the major, is one of many joyous romps.

Op. 33, No. 2, in E♭ ("The Joke") — *Allegro moderato, cantabile, Scherzo Allegro/Trio, Largo sostenuto, Presto.* There are many masterful touches in this quartet. The *Trio* demands that the first fiddle must slide on the E string to get the proper effect. The slow movement begins with a viola solo, accompanied only by the cello for eight measures. The "joke" is in the last movement, and it is only funny to an audience. The players, with music, in front of them, are not surprised. The opening theme of the movement is reprised at the end, but it is split up by changes of tempo and many rests. When a listener thinks it is finished, there is a three-measure general pause. The quartet ends on a phrase where the listener expects more will come.

Op. 33, No. 3, in C ("The Bird") — *Allegro moderato, Scherzando, (Allegro)/Trio, Adagio, Rondo (Presto)*. This is sheer pleasure all the way. The first movement and the slow movement are very beautiful. The *Scherzando* is played by everyone on the lowest string, and the *Trio*, from which the quartet may get its soubriquet, is a chirping duet for the violins. The Finale is a Hungarian Rondo, where everyone has fun.

Op. 33, No. 4, in B♭ — *Allegro moderato, Scherzo (Allegretto), Minore (Trio), Largo, Presto*. We do not understand why anyone would not like this work. It is relatively short, but it is worthwhile if only for the hilarious last movement. The first violin states the rollicking theme, then the cello plays melody for an E♭ episode, while second fiddle and viola relax playing accompaniment. Suddenly, the middle voices are called on to contribute extended passages in 16th notes. The movement ends with the first violin playing tricks with the theme, followed by *pizzicato* double-stops by all the players.

Op. 33, No. 5, in G — *Vivace assai, Largo (Cantabile), Scherzo (Allegro)/Trio, Finale (Allegretto)*. The slow movement is among the most beautiful Haydn provided. The *Finale* might have been the inspiration for the wonderful last movement of Mozart's K421.

Op. 33, No. 6, in D — *Vivace assai, Andante, Scherzo (Allegro)/Trio, Finale (Allegretto)*. The first movment is directed to be played at a very lively pace. Once we had a first violin who played it almost andante, and it worked. This is unusual, because most music drives the players to the "right" tempo, whether they can play all the notes or not. The serene *Andante* provides an opportunity to show the beauty of his instrumental tone. The *Finale* is a theme and variations.

Op. 42 in D Minor — *Andante ed Innocentemente, Minuetto (Allegretto)/Trio, Adagio e cantabile, Finale (Presto)*. What ever happened to the other five? This is a fine, melodic and relatively brief quartet that makes a good introduction for new quartet players.

The Haydn Quartets after the "Haydn" Quartets. From Op. 50 on, the Haydn quartets were written after the Mozart quartets dedicated to Haydn. Mozart was the first real peer Haydn encountered among his contemporaries. The Op. 50 set was dedicated to the cello-playing King of Prussia, and they are sometimes called the Prussian Quartets. There is no special accommodation to the cellist in these quartets.

Op. 50, No. 1, in B♭ — *Allegro, Adagio non lento, Poco Allegretto/Trio, Finale (Vivace).* The only technical problem in this comes in the *Trio,* where the first fiddle plays off the beat in answer to the second on the beat and an octave lower. The variations in the slow movement provide some solo opportunity for the second fiddle. The last movement is high-spirited.

Op. 50, No. 2, in C — *Vivace, Adagio cantabile, Minuetto (Allegretto)/Trio, Finale (Vivace assai).* Likely, well before this point in studying the Haydn quartets, one may wonder if he would be more appreciated if he had not produced so many individual masterpieces. This is yet another wonder. The second fiddle may want to suggest it for the solo beginning the slow movement. This also has a high-register solo for the cellist.

Op. 50, No. 3, in E♭ — *Allegro con brio, Andante più tosto Allegretto, Minuetto (Allegretto)/Trio, Finale (Presto).* Thoroughly interesting and enjoyable for each player, finishing with another joyous theme.

Op. 50, No. 4, in F♯ Minor — *Allegro spirituoso, Andante, Minuetto (Poco Allegretto)/Trio, Finale (Fugue).* This quartet provides the last instance of a fugal finale, great drama and much beauty. The minuet is in the major (six sharps), but it lies well. Haydn knew instrument capabilities. The slow movement, in the relative major of A, with an A minor interlude, is outstanding.

Op. 50, No. 5, in F ("A Dream") — *Allegro moderato, Adagio, Minuetto (Allegretto)/Trio, Finale (Vivace).* The "dream" nickname comes from the character of the *Adagio.* This has another happy conclusion. Players are cautioned to believe the *moderato* direction for the first movement, where I find it useful to count in 4/8 instead of 2/4.

Op. 50, No. 6, in D ("The Frog") — *Allegro, Poco Adagio,*

Minuetto (Allegretto)/Trio, Finale (Allegro con spirito). This is the only "Celebrated" quartet of the opus, and we cannot quarrel with the selection. Its name comes from the bariolage in the last movement. This might remind someone of frogs croaking, especially if it is played by amateurs. The slow movement is lovely.

Op. 51, "The Seven Last Words of Our Savior from the Cross." This was composed on commission for the Cadiz Cathedral as orchestral interludes for performance on Good Friday, with an Introduction and a concluding "Earthquake." Haydn arranged it for string quartet, and it is counted as seven quartets. This is interesting intellectually as the only instance of program music among Haydn's quartets and as a problem in playing seven successive slow movements. We never had enough intellectual interest to get past the second one of the slow movements. Excluding these, the Op. 1 and 2 and the (spurious) Op. 3 from the nominal 83 quartets of Haydn, we amateurs are still blessed with 58 Haydn masterpieces to work on.

The Tost Quartets, Op. 54, Op. 55, Op. 64. These twelve quartets were supposedly dedicated to Johann Tost, who by one account was a violinist in the Esterházy orchestra who married well and became a prosperous cloth merchant.

Op. 54, No. 1, in G — *Allegro con brio, Allegretto, Minuetto (Allegretto)/Trio, Finale (Presto).* Some people claim the Tost quartets are top heavy in first violin. We do not agree. The effect is fine.

Op. 54, No. 2, in C — *Vivace, Adagio, Minuetto (Allegretto)/Trio, Finale (Adagio/Presto).* One infers that Haydn was experimenting as he did continually throughout his lifetime. The first movement is very dramatic and the second a poem for violin and accompaniment. The last movement provides a treatment of one theme as an adagio and a presto. It takes work to bring it off.

Op. 54, No. 3, in E — *Allegro, Largo cantabile, Minuetto (Allegretto)/Trio, Presto.* We used to avoid this in our beginnings along with any works with more than three sharps or flats. The terror receded with experience. This is the first work in E since Op. 17, No. 1, but unlike it, there is no use of E minor. Instead, the slow movement is in A and A minor. A very pleasing quartet.

Op. 55, No. 1, in A — *Allegro, Adagio cantabile, Minuetto/Trio, Vivace.* This is an outstanding work. The first violin would be well advised to finger passages in the first movement and get acquainted with the very high notes in the *Trio*. The slow movement, in D, is opened by the second fiddle, and the beauty of the movement is superlative. We know that the Mozart K464 was the model for the Beethoven Op. 18, No. 5. We wonder if the Mozart quartet was not also the model for this one of Haydn's.

Op. 55, No. 2, in F Minor ("The Razor") — *Andante più tosto Allegretto, Allegro, Minuetto (Allegretto)/Trio, Presto*. The name is derived from the apocryphal story that Haydn told the English publisher Bland that he would trade his best quartet for a good razor. The best part of the quartet is the very funny finale, which is in the major. The first movement variations are interesting but not especially attractive — for Haydn.

Op. 55, No. 3, in B♭ — *Vivace assai, Adagio ma non troppo, Minuetto/Trio, Presto*. Every time we pull this out, someone remarks that we should play it more often.

Op. 64, No. 1, in C — *Allegro moderato, Minuetto (Allegretto ma non troppo)/Trio, Allegretto scherzando, Presto*. This is the orphan of the opus, the only one not "celebrated" by Moser and Dechert. People who hate to count slow movements need not worry here; there is none. It has some fine touches.

Op. 64, No. 2, in B Minor — *Allegro spirituoso, Adagio ma non troppo, Minuetto (Allegretto)/Trio, Presto*. The second great B minor quartet is capped with a very funny finale, ending in B major. The *Adagio*, in B major, is a masterpiece of serene beauty.

Op. 64, No. 3, in B♭ — *Vivace assai, Adagio, Minuetto (Allegretto)/Trio, Allegro con spirito*. Another delight. The slow movement, in E♭, has an extended section in the minor, six flats. The minuet is notable for its charm.

Op. 64, No. 4, in G — *Allegro con brio, Minuetto (Allegretto)/Trio, Adagio, Presto*. A beautiful quartet, especially the slow movement (in C).

Op. 64, No. 5, in D ("The Lark") — *Allegro moderato, Adagio cantabile, Minuetto (Allegretto)/Trio, Vivace*. The name comes from the soaring melody in the first movement. The slow movement is quite lovely. The last movement is often played as if it were a *perpetuo mobile*. Even if it is played cleanly at very fast speed, it loses impact in the minor key middle section. *Vivace* is not synonymous with *Prestissimo*.

Op. 64, No. 6, in E♭ — *Allegretto, Andante, Minuetto (Allegretto)/Trio, Presto.* This has a very pretty slow movement and one of many fine finales.

The "Apponyi" Quartets, Op. 71 and Op. 74 were dedicated to a Hungarian Count. The Op. 74 are in the "Celebrated" set; the Op. 71 are not. These provide more challenging parts for the lower strings than the Op. 64 set, and some of them have short introductions.

Op. 71, No. 1, in B♭ — *Allegro, Adagio, Minuetto (Allegretto)/Trio, Vivace.* This gets played more often than others simply because it is the first quartet in the volume. It is well worthwhile, but the reason for arranging the quartets in the Peters volumes passes our understanding.

Op. 71, No. 2, in D — *Adagio/Allegro, Andante cantabile, Minuetto (Allegro), Allegretto.* This has a four-measure introduction and a stepwise entry of instruments in the first movement. It is an interesting work.

Op. 71, No. 3, in E♭ — *Vivace, Andante con moto, Minuetto/Trio, Vivace.* The slow movement is one with variations in B♭ and B♭ minor. This is a device Haydn employed often.

Op. 74, No. 1, in C — *Allegro moderato, Andantino grazioso, Minuetto (Allegro)/Trio, Vivace.* This begins with a chord and a pause. It has a very charming slow movement.

Op. 74, No. 2, in F — *Allegro spirituoso, Andante grazioso, Minuetto (Allegro)/Trio, Presto.* This is a great quartet for getting acquainted with new players, especially a new second fiddle. It begins with a unison so there is no problem establishing the rhythm. The slow movement has a pattern that Haydn used earlier, e.g., in Op. 71, No. 3, where the tonic is B♭ but some of the variations are in B♭ Minor. In this instance, the melody in the minor is given to the second violin. It is a chance for the second fiddle to show beautiful tone. In spite of the five flats of the key, it lies well. The *Presto* is another rollicking Finale that leaves the players feeling good about their efforts.

Op. 74, No. 3, in G Minor ("The Rider") — *Allegro, Largo assai, Minuetto (Allegretto)/Trio, Allegro con brio.* The name of the quartet comes from the galloping syncopated rhythms of the last movement.

The *Largo*, in the related major key of E, is very beautiful. The entire quartet is outstanding among the long succession of masterpieces Haydn produced.

The Op. 76 quartets were dedicated to Count Erdödy, who was also a friend of Beethoven. This last set of six quartets is wonderful, with each one different from the others (as is true of any Haydn opus). We marvel that Haydn never repeated himself. Ideas flowed unimpeded throughout his life.

Op. 76, No. 1, in G — *Allegro con spirito, Adagio sostenuto, Minuetto (Presto)/Trio, Allegro ma non troppo.* After two measures of chords, the instruments enter individually beginning with the cello. The first violin completes the ensemble in the 12th measure, and it would be well for him to be in practice to handle the fiddling in store in the first movement. The slow movement is in C, serene and lovely. The *Trio* is outstanding and so is the finale. This is unusual in that it begins in G minor. The change to major near the end provides perfect contrast.

Op. 76, No. 2, in D Minor ("Quinten") — *Allegro, Andante, Allegro più tosto Allegretto, Minuetto (Allegro, ma non troppo)/Trio, Vivace assai.* The name comes from the use of falling fifths in the first movement (Schumann loved this motif, and it became a characteristic of his own compositions). The slow movement, in D, starts with the first violin playing a melody against pizzicato accompaniment, and it is very effective. The minuet and trio provide a fierce canon of the violins against the viola and cello. The trio, in the major, swells to a fortissimo. It is not at all pretty, nor must it have been intended to be. It is called "the witches minuet." The finale ends in D major.

Op. 76, No. 3, in C ("The Emperor") — *Allegro, Poco Adagio, cantabile, Minuetto (Allegro)/Trio, Presto.* I hope someday to play the first violin part in the first movement cleanly twice. If I can do it more than once at a quartet session, I will consider myself a competent player. The slow movement provides unorthodox variations on Haydn's anthem, *Gott erhalten Franz den Kaiser,* which later became the German national hymn, *Deutschland über Alles.* Thus, the eponym for this quartet. The theme is stated by the first violin, then it is played in turn by the second violin, accompanied only by the first, the cello in the second variation, and the viola in the third variation. The fourth variation provides the theme played by the first violin an octave higher with different harmonies. The unorthodox feature of this theme and variations is that the same theme is presented five times, but the accompaniment is varied. Like No. 1 of the set, the finale begins in the minor and ends in the major.

Op. 76, No. 4, in B♭ ("Sunrise") — *Allegro con spirito, Adagio, Minuetto (Allegro)/Trio, Allegro ma non troppo.* Haydn's inventiveness never flagged. The quartet likely gets its name from the long rising theme of the first movement. The slow movement, in E♭, is lovely. The last movement is very effective, with an episode in B♭ minor, then a change in tempo to *Più Allegro* climaxing in a *Presto.*

Op. 76, No. 5, in D ("with the Largo") — *Allegretto, Largo, Cantabile e mesto, Minuetto (Allegro)/Trio, Presto.* The first movement is a 6/8 tune with a variation in the minor. After the return to D major, the second violin has the responsibility of quickening the tempo to an *Allegro,* where it is better to start counting in twos toward the exciting finish. The *Largo* is in the remote key of F♯ (six sharps), which causes surprisingly little difficulty. The *Presto* is a fine conclusion.

Op. 76, No. 6, in E♭ ("with the Fantasia") — *Allegretto, Fantasia, Adagio, Minuetto (Presto)/Alternativo, Allegro spirituoso.* Once again, after theme and variations, the second violin changes tempo from a 2/4 (where we count in four) to an *Allegro* in the first movement. The *Fantasia* begins with no key signature at all, then it is marked in B major (five sharps). The *Alternativo* as trio stands the minuet theme on its head, with statements and responses by the part-players. The finale takes work to hold together. It is in 3/4, and it begins with three eighth notes, but it is too fast to count in 6/8.

The Last Quartets comprise the two of Op. 77 and the unfinished quartet. Haydn was about 70 years old when these were published. By this time, Haydn's only living peer was the young Beethoven, but these quartets are pure Haydn. Composers in succeeding generations, naturally, wrote in different styles. No one has approached Haydn in the number of masterpieces he produced, and few in consistency of quality.

Op. 77, No. 1, in G — *Allegro moderato, Adagio, Minuetto (Presto)/Trio, Vivace.* This is a joy to play for each part all the way through. The E♭ slow movement has placid beauty. There are many excursions in remote keys.

Op. 77, No. 2, in F—*Allegro moderato, Minuetto (Presto, ma non troppo)/Trio/Coda, Andante, Vivace assai.* This last complete Haydn quartet is representative of his work in that it is an individual masterpiece. There are no special technical problems, but the first violin has an extended passage in the slow movement in 64th notes. The "black" tends to daunt many first fiddles, but the section is not really difficult.

Op. 103, The Unfinished Quartet—*Andante grazioso, Minuetto/Trio.* The *Andante* is in B♭, but it changes to six flats and to four sharps before returning to the tonic. It is a remarkable composition in its harmonies. The minuet is in D minor with a trio in D major, and it is more conventional. From the minuet, one would guess that the key of the quartet would have been D minor; however, Haydn did not have the energy to write an opening movement and a finale. At the end, he appended the Song of the Old Man, "Gone is all my strength. Old and weak am I."

Paul Hindemith

Minimax Reportorium für Militärmusik für Streichquartett—*Armeemarsch 606*—*Der Hohenfurstenberger, Ouverture zu "Wasser-dichter und Vogelbaur"* (a play on von Suppé's "Poet and Peasant"), *Ein Abend an der Donauquelle, Intermezzo für zwei entfernte trompeten (Violine II und Viola aus der Ferne)* (two distant trumpets, second violin and viola), *Löwenzähnchen an Baches Rand, Konzert-walzer* (dandelions at the brookside), *Die beiden lustigen Mistfinken, Charakterstück, Solo für zwei Piccoloflöten, Alte Karbonaden, Marsch.* Hindemith was a prolific composer. The only quartet we have tried is this uncharacteristic spoof which he wrote for his own quartet, where he played viola and his brother, cello. The "Minimax" derives from the princely couple Wilhelmina and Maximilian; however, we confess that we miss most of the allusions. Imitations of an out-of-tune military band and quotations from other pieces (e.g., The Carnival of Venice and Beethoven's Fifth Symphony) make for great fun. The only difficult part technically is the "two merry ragamuffins," where the violins imitate piccolos by playing duet in fingered harmonics.

Felix Mendelssohn

Mendelssohn did some fine things in his lifetime. At 16 he composed a marvelous octet for double string quartet. At 26, he became conductor of the Leipzig Gewandhaus orchestra. Later he was a leader in reviving the popularity of the music of Bach. He wrote an estimable violin concerto, and he was much loved and respected during his short lifetime. The fine things he accomplished do not extend to his string quartets. (Here I must admit to prejudice. My first experience with Mendelssohn was playing second violin or viola parts of his Op. 44, No. 1, in D. Only Grieg's Op. 27—of quartets I have participated in—rivals the first movement for lack of ideas and taste, but the Grieg is more fun to play.) If Mendelssohn had stopped with one quartet, it would have been representative. Mendelssohn knew how to write quartets; he simply had little to say in the medium. The string quintets and the piano trios seem to this amateur player much more worthwhile; however, amateur quartet players will form their own judgments. There are people who love the quartets.

Op. 12 in E♭—*Adagio non troppo / Allegro non tardante, Canzonetta (Allegretto), Andante espressivo, Molto allegro e vivace.* This quartet was written two years after Op. 13. The high point of it is the G minor/G major *Canzonetta*, which a famous quartet used as an encore. From the players' standpoint, all have much work to do throughout this quartet and all of the others.

Op. 13 in A—*Adagio / Allegro vivace, Adagio non lento (cantabile), Intermezzo (Allegrettto con moto / Allegro di molto), Presto.* The work begins and ends with the *Adagio* in A, a quotation from a song, but most of it is in A minor. Those who enjoy Op. 12 should enjoy this. The writer likes it more, principally for the concluding *Presto*, which has a dramatic recitative for first fiddle near the end.

Op. 44, No. 1, in D—*Molto allegro vivace, Minuetto (Un poco Allegretto), Andante espressivo ma con moto, Presto con brio.* The first movement begins with second violin and viola sawing frantically and loudly on 16th note double-stops for 11 measures, trying unsuccessfully to drown out the maniacal voice of the first violin. From here on, there is no direction to go but up, and the movement ascends from the hysterical to the mulodramatic. The reward for persistence comes in the second movement, from which one may find himself humming the lovely theme for weeks after. The final two movements are "characteristic," craftmanship masquerading as art. (This quartet was a favorite of its composer!)

Op. 44, No. 2, in E Minor — *Allegro assai appassionato, Scherzo (Allegro di molto), Andante, Presto agitato.* This quartet aroused no ill temper. The *Scherzo*, in the major, is typical of Mendelssohn scherzi. The *Andante*, in G major, bears the note, *Dieses Stück darf durchaus nicht schleppend gespielt werden*, an instruction to the players not to drag the piece throughout. The *Andante* (4/4) begins with two measures of the second violin playing legato 16th note patterns, the viola eighths and the cello whole notes before the first violin announces the theme. If one but tells the second fiddle and violist about this, it relieves anxiety and promotes nearly perfect ensemble. We discovered this after many false starts where the second fiddle thought he was playing too fast and the violist at half speed. It is worthwhile penciling notes in the parts.

Op. 44, No. 3, in E♭ — *Allegro vivace, Scherzo (Allegro leggiero vivace), Adagio non troppo, Molto allegro con fuoco.* This begins dramatically and leaves its promise unfulfilled.

Op. 80 in F Minor — *Allegro vivace assai/Presto, Allegro assai, Adagio, Finale (Allegro molto).* This starts unpromisingly with everyone sawing away at 16ths in cut-time, a tremolo effect, but it then gets interesting. The second movement (F minor) is arresting. The *Adagio* (A♭) is unremarkable. The last movement is exciting. Overall, this writer would choose this and the Op. 13 as the best of these quartets.

Op. 81, Four pieces for string quartet — Theme and Variations *(Andante sostenuto)* in E, *Scherzo (Allegro leggiero)* in A Minor, *Capriccio (Allegro con moto/Allegro fugato, assai vivace)* in E minor, *Fuga (a tempo ordinario)* (E♭). This is a posthumous collection of isolated movements. The ITSQ never bothered with it.

Wolfgang Amadeus Mozart

The Juvenile Quartets. Mozart wrote two sets of quartets when he was a teenager following a single quartet, K80. They are not nearly as interesting as early Haydn or mature Mozart. In its beginnings, the Ill Tempered String Quartet might have been advised to begin with early Mozart or Haydn quartets to develop ensemble and style. Instead, the quartet tried to play more difficult—and interesting—works. The early Mozart quartets are usually read through once. What is played is a group decision, and the lower strings, especially, look for compositions that provide interest and technical challenge beyond these. The early quartets were written when Mozart was 16 and 17 years old. The first of the quartets dedicated to Haydn was written when he had the benefit of studying the Haydn masterpieces of Op. 33.

K155 in D—*Allegro moderato, Andante, Molto Allegro.*

K156 in G—*Presto, Adagio, Tempo di Minuetto.*

K157 in C—*Allegro, Andante, Presto.* This is one of the most effective of the early quartets. The first movement is great fun, and the slow movement is very pretty.

K158 in F—*Allegro, Andante, un poco Allegretto, Tempo di Minuetto.*

K159 in B♭—*Andante grazioso, Allegro, Rondo (Allegro grazioso).*

K160 in E♭—*Allegro, Un poco adagio, Presto.*

K168 in F—*Allegro, Andante, Minuetto/Trio, Fuga (Allegro).*

K169 in A—*Molto allegro, Andante, Minuetto/Trio, Rondo (Allegro).*

K170 in C—*Andante, Minuetto/Trio, Poco adagio, Rondo (Allegro).*

K171 in E♭—*Adagio/Allegro assai, Minuetto/Trio, Andante/Allegro assai.*

K172 in B♭—*Allegro spirituoso, Adagio, Men/trio, Allegro assai.*

K173 in D Minor—*Allegro ma molto moderato, Andantino grazioso, Minuetto/Trio, Fuga (Allegro).*

Mozart's Maturity: "The Haydn Quartets." The six quartets, K387 through K465, were dedicated to Josef Haydn, who, pensioned from his position as music director for the Esterházys, had moved to Vienna.

NOTES ON THE LITERATURE

Collectively, they are referred to as "The Haydn Quartets," which causes surprisingly little confusion. At the time they were written, Mozart and Haydn had become friends, and the younger man was well acquainted with Haydn's Op. 33. There is an authenticated story about a private quartet session where Haydn played the first violin, Dittersdorf second, Mozart viola and Wanhal cello. The editors of the Peters edition of the Mozart quartets were Andreas Moser and Hugo Becker (1863–1941). Becker was a famous cello soloist in his time as well s a quartet cellist.

K387 in G—*Allegro vivace assai, Minuetto/Trio, Andante cantabile, Molto Allegro.* The first movement of this has always struck me as pleasant but banal. The minuet requires that the players have bow and string ready to play during rests and pay attention to the alternation of forte and piano passages. The theme is passed from one instrument to another in midsyllable, as it were. If one instrument were allowed to complete a phrase, there would be less tension and a lesser effect. The G minor *Trio* begins with everyone on lowest string, and it is very effective. We found it useful to count the *Andante* in six beats to the measure. The last movement is begun by the second violin, who has the hardest job counting. It should be played two beats to the measure.

K421 in D Minor—*Allegro, Andante (F), Minuetto/Trio, Allegretto ma non troppo.* This is a quartet that the violist, especially, will want to play, but everyone has interesting problems. The *Trio* has an off-beat-stress first violin solo to *pizzicato* accompaniment by the lower strings. The violist joins the first violin at an octave lower during the second repeat. The *Andante* is in the relative major, F, and it is pleasant and not difficult. The Breitkopf and Härtel version gives *Allegro non troppo* for the last movement, where the viola has a wonderful solo in one of the variations. The quartet ends in a *Più allegro* major, where the Peters editors specified a downbow spiccato for triplets. This is awkward. The second violin has some cross rhythms in one of the variations, and these are difficult to sight-read.

K428 in E♭—*Allegro non troppo, Andante con moto, Minuetto/Trio, Allegro vivace.* Whenever we played this, we would wonder why we had not played it more often. It has marvelous parts for all the players. The *Andante,* in A♭, is outstanding, reminiscent of the slow movement in Haydn Op. 20, No.1.

125

K458 in B♭ (Hunt) — *Allegro vivace assai, Minuetto/Trio, Adagio, Allegro assai.* This is a joy throughout. The *Adagio,* in E♭, is the only movement where counting can be a problem.

K464 in A — *Allegro, Minuetto/Trio, Andante, Allegro.* The editors of the Peters edition saw fit to reverse the order of the *Minuetto/Trio* and *Andante,* which are presented in the correct — as Mozart wrote it — order by Breitkopf and Härtel and in the Schirmer edition. I have noted in the parts of the Peters edition that the *Andante* should be played as the third movement. In common with Beethoven's taste, this is one of my favorite Mozart quartets. The *Andante,* in D with a D minor interlude, should be counted 4/8 and all the repeats honored so its end is delayed as long as possible. The movement ends with a "drum beat motif," introduced by the cello, passed on to the other instruments and finally restated by the cello. The Peters edition calls the last movement cut-time and *Allegro non troppo.* The cut-time is appropriate, especially in the sections where whole note chords are played by the quartet.

K465 in C ("Dissonance") — *Adagio/Allegro, Andante cantabile, Minuetto/Trio, Allegro.* This is a favorite quartet among amateurs. The nickname comes from the dissonances in the 22 measure *Adagio,* which we have found useful to count in six instead of 3/4 as written. The cello begins and sets the pulse.

K499 in D ("Hoffmeister") — *Allegretto, Minuetto/Trio, Adagio (G), Allegro.* This great quartet is the orphan, dedicated neither to Haydn nor the King of Prussia. Supposedly it was dedicated to Franz Anton Hoffmeister, a composer and music dealer, who founded a music publishing firm about 1800 which was a predecessor to C.F. Peters and Sons. The *Adagio,* in G, is among the finest of the many very beautiful ones Mozart wrote.

K546, Adagio and Fugue (1788) — This appears in the second Mozart volume from Peters, along with the early quartets, the flute quartets, *Eine kleine Nachtmusik,* and the oboe quartet. The fugue was Mozart's transcription of an earlier version for two pianos, and the *Adagio* was added. It is well worth having.

K575 in D (1789) — *Allegretto, Andante (A), Minuetto/Trio Allegretto.* This is the first of the quartets dedicated to King Friedrich Wilhelm II of Prussia, an avid cellist and nephew of Frederick the

Great. Mozart set himself the problem of writing quartets which would have a very melodic and prominent cello part. His solution was to provide solo passages for all the parts, so these are very satisfying to assertive second fiddles and violists. The cellist has many opportunities to sing out in the tenor register.

K589 in B♭ (1790) — *Allegro, Larghetto (E♭), Minuetto/Trio, Allegro assai.* This marvelous quartet is very effective and not at all difficult until one comes to the *Trio.* Unless the first violin is very good, we recommend that time be spent in studying this and putting in fingerings. The minuet is marked *moderato,* and this should be observed. Success in not butchering the *Trio* came after many tries and much study. We still look forward to playing it well.

K590 in F (1790) — *Allegro moderato, Allegretto (Andante) in C, Minuetto/Trio, Allegro.* This last of Mozart's string quartets has no great problems. A violist who is not alert at the end can ruin the effect by coming in late with the last statement of the theme. Fortunately, we never recorded how often I did this.

Sergei Prokofiev

Op. 50 in B Minor — *Allegro, Andante moto, Andante.* We have played only this first quartet so far, and that only once. It has very lyrical passages. The violist stopped the quartet on the first page and exclaimed, "It sounds just like the theme from *Romeo and Juliet!*" We approximated a version of the ballet theme, which is quite different, but she was unconvinced. The conclusion was the Prokofiev's music is original and his characteristics are easily recognizable in unfamiliar works.

Op. 92 in F — *Allegro moderato, Adagio, Allegro.* This was written in the Caucasus in 1942. It is based on folk tunes of that region.

Maurice Ravel

Quartet in F — *Allegro moderato (Très doux), Assez vif — Très rythmé, Très lent, Vif et Agité.* This is a wonderful quartet to study.

It sounds great, and the first movement is not very difficult. From there on, it requires better players than we are now.

Franz Peter Schubert

Schubert played viola in his family quartet in his boyhood. His father was the cellist. Following is a table of Schubert's string quartets:

No.	Date	Key	P	Opus	D no.
1	1812	B♭	-	-	18
2	1812	C	-	-	32
3	1813	B♭	-	-	36
4	1813	C	-	-	46
5	1813	B♭	-	-	68
6	1813	D	-	-	74
7	1814	D	II	-	94
8	1814	B♭	II	168	112
9	1815	G Min.	II	-	173
10	c.1813	E♭	I	125#1	87
11	c.1817	E	I	125#2	353
12	1820	C Min.	II	-	703
13	1824	A Min.	I	29	804
14	1826	D Min.	I	-	810
15	1826	G	II	161	887

"P" shows the volume of the Peters edition coverage of the last nine quartets.

No. 1 in B♭—*Andante, Presto vivace, Minuetto/Trio, Presto.*

No. 2 in C—*Presto, Minuetto/Trio.*

No. 3 in B♭, D36-*Allegro, Andante, Minuetto/Trio, Allegretto.*

No. 4 in C, D46—*Adagio, Andante con moto, Minuetto/Trio, Allegro.*

No. 5 in B♭, D68—*Allegro, Allegro.* Someone suggested in print that these two movements were intended to be played before and after the two movements of Haydn's Op. 103, which begins with an *Andante* in B♭. The Haydn movement, judging from its *Minuet* and *Trio* keys probably would have been in D minor, so the suggestion is hard to credit.

No. 6 in D, D74—*Allegro ma non troppo, Andante, Minuetto/Trio, Allegro.* Someone once brought around copies of the first six, and we played them—once. Like early Mozart, it is probably something to do so that you can say you have.

No. 7 in D, D94—*Allegro, Andante con moto, Minuetto/Trio, Presto.* This is very lyrical.

No. 8 in B♭, Op. 168, D112—*Allegro ma non troppo, Andante sostenuto, Minuetto/Trio, Presto.* The opus number is meaningless. Like all but one Schubert quartet, it was published posthumously. The quartet has some fine lyrical and dramatic moments.

No. 9 in G Minor, D173—*Allegro con brio, Andantino, Minuetto/Trio, Allegro.* This is a favorite from start to finish. The *Andantino* is very lyrical. The 16th note passages in the last movement reveal whether or not the players practice.

No. 10 in E♭, Op. 125, No. 1, D 87—*Allegro moderato, Scherzo (Prestissimo)/Trio, Adagio, Allegro.* Many of my quartet companions like this very much. I find it banal. I am willing to play it, but I never suggest it. This is actually the earliest quartet in the Peters volumes, written when the composer was 16.

No. 11 in E, D353, Op. 125, No. 2—*Allegro con fuoco, Andante, Minuetto/Trio, Rondo (Allegro vivace).* This has its moments, especially in the dramatic first movement, where the first fiddle has plenty of work at high altitude.

No. 12 in C Minor, D703 ("Quartettsatz")—*Allegro assai.* The "Quartet Movement" seems universally referred to in German, even by English-only speakers. This is the beginning of the masterpieces. A fragment of the second movement has survived, and it has been recorded by a major professional string quartet. One wonders why. Nevertheless, the movement is wonderful, combining the dramatic and the lyrical. The only difficult part is that of the first violin.

No. 13 in A Minor, Op. 29, D804—*Allegro ma non troppo, Andante, Minuetto/Trio, Allegro moderato.* This is a wonderful quartet that looks very easy but has some traps, especially the finale. It was the only one of Schubert's quartets published in his brief lifetime, hence the low opus number. The second movement, *Andante* (cut-time), reuses a familiar theme from other Schubert works, and impromptu for piano and the suite of incidental music from Rosamunde (stuttering is not plagiarism). One may want to note that the first section is not repeated. Sextuplet 16th runs for all the players—at different places—make it advantageous to count in 4/4 or even a fast 8/8 when these occur. The minuet is an *Allegretto* in the usual 3/4 with a *Trio* in the major. The *Allegro moderato* finale, 2/4, in A major tempts the first fiddle to start at too fast a pace, and he and everyone else goes out of control later on when the chromatic sextuplets begin. After years of desperate—mostly losing—gambles on getting through this movement, we discovered that it can be handled by counting a moderate 4/8 instead of 2/4, then the sextuplets are played like double triplets—or at least thought of that way.

No. 14 in D Minor, D810 ("Death and the Maiden")—*Allegro, Andante con moto, Scherzo, Presto.* It used to be—and perhaps still is—that any Air Force personnel checking out a parachute would be assured by any supply sergeant anywhere that it was guaranteed—if it doesn't work it will be cheerfully exchanged for another. The supplier invariably thought himself an original wit. Similarly, there are few amateur readings of "Death and the Maiden" where someone does not assert that the chastity of the maiden has been compromised. The title comes from the *Andante,* which used the theme from the song, *Der Tod und das Mädchen,* as a basis for variations in G minor. The quartet is a joy to read, to play and to hear from beginning to end. Some players like to skip repeats in Schubert, feeling the quartets are too prolix, but we recommend that all repeats be observed so that the end of the quartet can be delayed as long as possible. The return of the minor after the G major variations in the *Andante,* provides eight measures which are played pianissimo the first time through then swell to an fortissimo the second time. The effect is magnificent. The quartet finishes with a prestissimo at triple forte. The quartet "lies well for the players," challenging, superbly effective and not overly difficult.

No. 15 in G, D887, Op. 161—*Allegro molto moderato, Andante un poco moto, Scherzo (Allegro vivace)/Trio, Allegro vivace.* We found to our surprise that the first two movements can be counted with eighth notes about the same speed. The quartet is long, gorgeous and exciting. We found an advantage in counting the first movement 6/8 instead of 3/4. The character of this quartet seems different from anything that had come before it, even granting the individuality of all his works. In the last movement, especially, it is a "finger-buster," but it is worthwhile getting in training for it.

Robert Schumann

The Op. 41 Quartets. Schumann decided to write string quartets in 1842 after studying the Haydn quartets. The quartets of this opus were turned out within a few weeks; however, he had a well-prepared mind. We do not understand the criticism sometimes voiced that the quartets are too "pianistic." We believe this criticism, if valid, might apply more appropriately to Beethoven, who is considered above criticism. The quartets take practice, but they are worth any effort needed.

Op. 41, No. 1, in A Minor—*Introduzione (Andante espressivo)/Allegro, Scherzo (Presto)/Intermezzo, Adagio, Presto.* The quartet begins 2/4, then a *stringendo* passage leads to a 6/8, which one counts in 2 most of the way, as if there were pairs of triplets in a measure. The lively *Scherzo* flanks an effective cut time *Intermezzo.* The *Adagio* is a beautiful movement which requires practice counting. I begin in 8 and switch to 16 beats to a measure when necessary. The concluding *Presto* is exciting, with an interesting *Moderato* in the major inserted for contrast.

Op. 41, No. 2, in F—*Allegro vivace, Andante quasi, Variazioni/ Coda, Scherzo (Presto)/Trio (L'istesso tempo)/Coda, Allegro molto vivace.* This is difficult sight-reading, especially the ladder-theme in the last movement, but it holds together well. There is no mistaking Schumann's music for that by anyone else. We love it.

Op. 41, No. 3, in A—*Andante espressivo/Allegro molto moderato, Assai agitato, Adagio molto, Finale (Allegro molto vivace/Quasi Trio).* This last quartet leaves us wishing Schumann had emulated Haydn to the extent of writing at least three more quartets. The off-beat accompaniments in the first movement take some practice. The second movement has many variations not marked as such. Instead they are identified by changes in tempo. The *Adagio molto,* has a magnificent part for viola in passages where it answers the first violin. The last movement was called "Schumannized Bach" by Robert Haven

Schauffler. There are many modulations and changes in key signature. The overall effect is like one of the happy Haydn finales.

Dmitry Shostakovich

Op. 49 in C—*Moderato, Moderato, Allegro molto, Allegro*. This is the only one of the 15 in many home libraries and the only one we have played so far. The first violin must be comfortable in high positions. The violist has a wonderful solo in the second movement.

Jean Sibelius

Op. 56 in D Minor ("Voces Intimae")—*Andante/Allegro molto moderato, Vivace, Adagio di molto, Allegretto, Allegro*. This has held a place in the literature. It does not seem to be difficult, but our experience with it is very limited.

Bedřich Smetana

Quartet No. 1, Op. 115, in E Minor ("From My Life")—*Allegro vivo appassionato, Allegro moderato à la Polka, Largo sostenuto, Vivace*. This begins with a solo for viola, which has a challenging part throughout. (Dvořák played the viola in the first reading of the quartet.) The second movement *Polka* has verve and charm. The *Largo* begins with a cadenza for cello. It is one of the most beautiful and affecting in the romantic literature. The last movement, mostly in E major, is the most difficult. It ends poignantly in the minor with a reprise of themes from the earlier movements. A high E sustained over a tremolo indicates the deafness of the composer. (Smetana wrote a second quartet in D minor, published posthumously, but we have not even heard it yet.)

Sergei Taneyev

Op. 7, No. 3 — *Allegro, Andantino grazioso.* This is a cyclic composition. The eight variations introduced in the second movement lead to a reprise of the beginning. It was enjoyed by all the players and presented no difficulties in a first reading.

Peter Ilyich Tchaikovsky

Op. 11 in D — *Moderato e semplice, Andante cantabile, Scherzo/Allegro non tanto e con fuoco/Trio, Allegro giusto.* Most of our Tchaikovsky experience has been with this quartet. One day we will get the courage to violate the direction and play the famous *Andante cantabile* without the mutes. The other movements have much to recommend them.

Op. 22 in F — *Adagio/Moderato assai, quasi andantino, Allegro giusto, Andante, ma non tanto, Allegro con moto.* We wait for an intrepid violinist to suggest this. Meanwhile, we work on the first violin part. It will be beautiful. Besides, we have a compelling need to play it; the music is expensive!

Op. 30 in E♭ Minor — *Andante sostenuto/Allegro moderato, Allegretto vivo e scherzando, Andante funebre e doloroso, ma con moto, Allegro risoluto.* We have worked up courage to play this a few times, undaunted by the key. It has gorgeous themes. We are entranced by the directions for the slow movement, which we interpret as meaning "dirge-like and sorrowfully" as at the funeral of someone we liked. Had anyone marked a movement, *Funebre e giocoso*?

Giuseppe Verdi

Quartet in E Minor — *Allegro, Andantino, Prestissimo, Scherzo-Fuga.* Anyone who has played a Verdi overture in an orchestra or who has listened to his music can recognize the mastery evident in this quartet. It is more dramatic than lyrical, save for the second movement, where the direction *con eleganza*, is provided. Considering that Verdi grew rich and famous from his marvelous operas, the lament of one chamber music fanatic that he might have contributed more to our literature had he not "wasted time" on opera is indefensible.

Why no **Zemlinsky?** Even the not-too-attentive reader will have noticed that a lot of the literature has been omitted. A crafty author must leave open the possibility of a second edition; however, venality is not the reason. We can only describe our own experience, and that does not include Zemlinsky, Rochberg and *most other writers* of string quartets. Our own experience is eclectic and (even) haphazard. Impressions of a quartet depend on what seat we occupy. I have played first violin, second violin and viola in several quartets at different times but only one part in others. The experience varies with the competence of the other three players as well as the understanding among them. One combination of players may work, and another, differing by only one person, may not.

XIII. Expansion and Contraction

Sometimes a congenial quartet of players will be able to meet regularly—many try for once a week—for some months. Inevitably, however, the services of one or more of these stalwarts is lost for a week, a month or longer. For this reason, advice was given above that a list of about 20 players should be maintained. The string quartet is a nearly perfect medium for chamber music players, and it has the advantage of being eminently practical for the amateur player. Amateur and semiprofessional orchestras exist in large numbers, but these must meet for rehearsals at regular times and days. They involve large numbers of individuals who must coordinate their schedules to that of the group and the conductor. The string quartet, in comparison, can arrange to meet on different days to accommodate personal and business schedules of the players.

Where the same group of four or five is able to meet regularly over an extended period of time, it is politic to maintain good relations with those others on the list by inviting them occasionally to expand the quartet to a quintet. One year, a "regular" member of the writer's quartet, a violin player, had a physical disability which limited the length of time he could play comfortably. For this protracted period, a quartet was arranged with the understanding that the infirm player would be notified of time and place and could play part of the evening, the entire session or not at all, at his option. If he attended, one of the violinists would change to viola for quintets.

When a violist from another state contacted one of us through the ACMP listing before an extended business trip in our area, he was invited to play quintets with the quartet already scheduled. One may want to get in a few extra sessions with the "alternates" to maintain an average for the times one is called away as well as to keep the relationships current. The extra sessions provide opportunity to try a different part, if one is a violinist-violist, as well as to enjoy a different quality of experience.

It sometimes happens that only two other players can be procured for a session or that a last minute emergency prevents one of the quartet from honoring his commitment or causes him to be an hour or more late. For these reasons it is essential that the host's library contains quintets and trios for various combinations. In addition to—and perhaps overriding—the practical logistic considerations there are fine compositions for string duos, trios and quartets, and these provide different technical challenges to the players than quartets as well as a different sonority. The Mozart quintets for two violins, two violas and cello are regarded even more highly than his string quartets, and his Divertimento, K563, for violin, viola and cello is acknowledged as a masterpiece. Some of the cognoscenti proclaim the Schubert quintet with two cellos, Op. 163, to be the greatest chamber work extant. There is great music available in forms other than the standard string quartet, although there is not as much of it.

Violin–Viola–Cello

If a violinist is the person missing or one of the violinists can substitute for a missing violist—or if one simply feels like exploring the trio literature—there is a fine literature for this combination. There are two string trios, both in Bb, written by the teen-aged Schubert. One of them is a single movement (D471), and it is often played while waiting for a late violinist or violist to appear. It is a gem of a composition, with beautiful parts for the three instruments, and it is not difficult. The other trio (D581), in the conventional four movements, is quite different in mood. Initial difficulties with the offbeat rhythms of the opening *Allegro moderato* and the *Andante* which follows it disappeared when it was decided to count both of these movements in a fast eight beats. The violin is dominant in this string trio, but the viola is rewarded with the melody in the *Trio* of the third movement.

The Mozart Divertimento in Eb, K563, is his longest chamber work in number of movements (six) and in number of measures (count them). This was among Mozart's last chamber music compositions, and he was in difficult financial straits at the time. The music does not convey his distress; it is a pure joy to play as well as hear. It is worth the effort for all three players to study their parts before trying to read them. The first movement contains chromatic passages that should be fingered. At the end of the first movement, most cellists who are reading the Peters edition have a problem with an extended passage in tenor clef that goes lower than cellists are used to.

By the time Mozart wrote this trio, the term "divertimento" was in disuse. In spite of its name, which suggests a piece written for use as background music at a garden party, this is a marvelous piece of music, ranking with Mozart's great quartets and quintets. Those who play both violin and viola will want to make an opportunity to play both parts.

Beethoven, too, wrote a six-movement piece for this composition. The *Serenade,* Op. 8, could be considered an early example of a cyclic composition, because the march theme of the first movement is recapitulated in the last movement. In addition, there are Op. 3, which is pleasant but uses a lot of part-doubling in octaves, and the three trios of Op. 9. These are more interesting, and the Op. 9, No. 3, in C minor is a masterpiece which can stand comparison with the quartets.

The Dohnányi *Serenade* for string trio, Op. 10, is another favorite. This has challenging parts for all three instruments and requires practice for good ensemble. The violist has a marvelous time in the second movement, first playing an extended solo, then running off arpeggios. Like the Beethoven *Serenade,* this provides a recapitulation of the opening march at the end. Several other string trios are available, and the combination can invite a pianist for the Mozart piano quartets or a flutist for his flute quartets. The Taneyev Op. 31 is another very gratifying string trio. The violist, as the only "middle voice" in a trio, has a more challenging part than in many quartets. Ensemble for all three players may be more difficult than in quartets, because the "clues" furnished by the fourth player are missing.

Two Violins–Viola

For occasions when the cellist is late, the Dvořák *Terzetto*, Op. 74, is a delightful way to pass the time. The first movement has been played much more often than the whole work, because it has been used principally for this purpose. Another interesting piece is the Taneyev Op. 21. (Sergei Ivanovich Taneyev, 1856–1915, was a Russian composer who published six string quartets and three string quintets, some of which are available.)

The Beethoven Op. 25, *Trio for Flute, Violin and Viola,* can be played by two violins and viola. It sounds better with the original instrumentation, but it is worthwhile considering the limited repertory. There is enough literature to play for a couple of evenings, but some might prefer to play duos if a cellist is unobtainable.

String Duos

If one player comes early — or two are late — it is worthwhile to have string duos in the library. There are many duets for two violins, but the contrast in tone and increased compass of duos for violin and viola somehow make them seem more like chamber music. These are worthwhile exploring in addition to quartets in a separate evening. The Mozart duos for violin and viola, K423 in G and K424 in B♭, are challenging, reasonably even in distribution of melodic material, and very satisfying. They require good rhythm, for a duo contains fewer of the clues available to a player in larger ensembles. If the instruments are playing a theme together, most of the time it is a good indication one of them is lost. Duos by Bruni for this combination have even distribution of melody. They are tuneful and interesting. (Antoine-Bartholemy Bruni reportedly served the French Revolution in 1789 by evaluating the instruments confiscated from the nobility.)

The *Passacaglia* by Handel-Halvorsen is available, both for violin-viola and violin-cello, and this is exciting. There are several other works available for violin-cello, including eight duos by Glière, which we recommend highly, Ravel, and Carl Stamitz. The Beethoven *Duet for Viola and Cello and Obbligato Eyeglasses,* WoOp. 32, has interesting sonorities. (WoOp is a listing of Beethoven work *without* *op*us numbers.) Beethoven wrote this for two amateur friends, who were "four-eyed," if not forewarned. Our experience with violin-cello or viola-cello duos is limited to the instances when one player comes early or other players are late, because we prefer to explore the rich piano trio literature or play string trios for an entire evening session.

String Quintets

There are many marvelous pieces for string quintets. Adding a second viola, a second cello or a double bass to a quartet changes the sonorities and sets up different possibilities of relationships between the players. For simplicity in exposition, the different types of quintets will be designated viola quintets, cello quintets, and so on, to denote the instrument added to the standard string quartet. Most of the famous ones are viola quintets, although the absolute count might be confounded by more than 100 written by Boccherini for two cellos. An early Dvořák quintet, Op. 77, was written as a double bass quintet. (Bass parts can be played by a second cello, although this changes the sound. Bass parts are written an octave higher than they are played.)

The Mozart viola quintets include an early work, K174 in B♭, K406 in C minor, which he arranged from a wind octet (K388), K515 in C, K516 in G minor, K593 in D and K614 in E♭. The quintets contain magnificent music. Beethoven's Op. 29 in C is less popular than Mozart's, and his other quintets, one (Op. 104) a rescoring of his Op.1, No. 3, piano trio, are rarely played. (He undertook Op. 104 on learning that someone else had published an inept string quintet version of his piano trio.)

The Schubert cello quintet in C is a gem of the literature. A practical problem in playing it at home, providing it can be played through in a reasonable time, is that one should have at least two other cello quintets available to keep the second cellist happy and occupied for the rest of the evening. (In some years, we had a player who was very competent on violin, viola and cello, so we could play it whenever we pleased and fill out the evening with viola quintets.) Boccherini and some others are possible.

There are two Mendelssohn viola quintets, Op. 18 in A and Op. 87 in B♭. These have good parts for all the players. The second of them has an extraordinarily beautiful slow movement. There are two fine Brahms viola quintets, Op. 88 in F and Op 111 in G. The Dvořák viola quintet, Op. 97 in E♭, is one where anyone who plays viola will want to grab for the *second* viola part. Unlike many viola quintets, where the second viola is paired with the first viola and the cello, this part is often the leader in the quintet. In spite of passages in A♭ minor (seven flats!) all the players enjoy it.

Piano Trios

Most piano trios were written for piano, violin and cello. This became a very popular combination for amateur music-making during the last half of the 18th century when the piano supplanted the harpsichord. The popularity of this form has continued to the present day, and the volume of the literature is only exceeded by that for string quartets. Haydn and Mozart wrote many piano trios. Beethoven's first published works were piano trios, and he produced several others. The Op. 11 is for B♭ clarinet instead of violin, but a version is provided for violin. Op. 70, No. 1, in D is known as "the Ghost" and Op 97 in B♭ as "the Archduke." Schubert provided two piano trios, Op. 99 in B♭ and Op. 100 in E♭, which are quite different from each other. In addition, there is a trio movement, a nocturne in B♭, which is very beautiful.

Mendelssohn's piano trios, Op. 49 in D minor and Op. 66 in C minor are popular, the first more so. The Smetana piano trio in G minor, Op. 15, has a difficult and rhapsodic first movement, but it is worth the effort to cope with and overcome the difficulty. The Dvořák piano trios are beautiful music. The Op. 90 in E minor is called the "Dumky Trio," because it uses the Czech form contrasting slow and fast sections. (The *Andante* of his Op. 51 string quartet is called a Dumka.)

The piano trio of Anton Arensky (1859–1904) has beautiful romantic themes. There are trios by Brahms, Tchaikovsky, Chopin, Rachmaninoff, Schumann, Glinka, and nearly all the great and near-great composers, and the range of difficulty is wide. Piano trios are very satisfying for the violinist and cellist. The balances in home music — but not the tone — may be helped by the relatively poor quality of most living room pianos, spinets instead of concert grands.

Piano Quartets

Mozart provided two fine quartets for piano, violin, viola and cello, K478 and K493. Beethoven wrote two juvenile piano quartets, with which we have never bothered. Schubert provided an *Adagio* and *Rondo Concertante*. There is one by Schumann, Op. 47, which is sometimes criticised for a passage where the composer directed the cellist to tune his C string lower in order to get a B♭ octave. Nonetheless, it is a remarkable piece of music which may bear repeated hearing better than the more familiar piano quintet. There are three Brahms piano quartets, and these require excellent players. They are well worth the work they require. Dvořák published two piano quartets, and many other composers have used this form.

Piano Quintets

Mozart and Beethoven wrote quintets for piano and winds. A version of the Mozart quintet, K452, is available for piano and string quartet. As might be expected, it is a wonderful piece the way Mozart wrote it and unsatisfactory in the strings version. The first great quintet for piano and strings was that of Schumann, Op. 44 in E♭. The Dvořák Op. 81 in A is another magnificent work, with beautiful Slavonic themes. Other piano quintets are those by Brahms, Franck and Shostakovich. Piano quintets, if played at all by amateurs, are usually worked up to accommodate a pianist who wants to try one. The famous Schubert "Trout" quintet is scored for piano, violin, viola, cello and double bass. The notes can be played using a second cello for the bass, but the music suffers.

Other Hetero Instrument Compositions

The Mozart trio K498 was written for B♭ clarinet, viola and piano. This can be played with a violin in place of the clarinet, but it loses in effect thereby. If it is played by violin, viola and piano, they can fill out the evening with the Mozart *Sinfonia Concertante,* K364.

The clarinet is a transposing instrument, with the commonly available instruments being B♭ or A. These are not interconvertible any more than are violin and viola. Music for the B♭ clarinet that is written in B♭ for strings is written in C for the wind instrument. Similarly, the key of C for an A clarinet is written in A (three sharps) for strings. Thus, the B♭ clarinet is used mostly for the flat keys and the other for sharp keys. Professional players must own both instruments, and an orchestra clarinet player may change from one to the other during one composition. Amateur clarinet players usually own only a B♭ instrument. It would be helpful if music lists specified which clarinet is needed or, at least, provided the tonic key of the composition as a clue.

The Mozart clarinet quintet, K581, is in A and requires an A clarinet. A version of this is available for B♭ clarinet in which the string parts are transposed up a half-tone to B♭. This is more difficult for the string players, who must negotiate passages in B♭ minor (five flats) instead of A minor (no sharps or flats), but the sheet music is much less expensive than a new clarinet. The Brahms clarinet quintet, Op. 115, is written for an A clarinet, in B minor, and a C minor version is available for B♭ clarinet.

Flutes and oboes are not transposing instruments. The Beethoven Op. 25 trio is fun to play when a flute is available, and there are flute quartets by Mozart and others. Horns are transposing instruments, and these are used in chamber music. The Mozart horn quintet, K407, is unusual because it is scored for one violin, two violas and cello as the strings. A transcription uses a cello as the substitute for the horn, but its music is written in the treble clef.

Transcriptions

No thunder will roll indicating divine displeasure at the substitution of a violin for a clarinet or oboe. There are no rules prohibiting this or other kinds of unnatural acts in the privacy of the home. The only penalty endured is that the transcription never sounds "right"; the enjoyment of the players is limited. Even the often-played K406 viola quintet, which was transcribed by Mozart himself from his K387 wind octet, does not sound as good as the wind version. It is enjoyable to the string players, but it is inferior to the string quintets which followed.

Playing transcriptions is not nearly so heinous a violation of the spirit of chamber music as part doubling, where two players will read the same part, transforming a string quartet into an unbalanced monstrosity. This is sometimes attempted where the number of players exceeds the number of parts in order to let everyone play. The experience is dismal. No storms have occurred during the very few times the writer has been exposed to this practice, but he was always looking out the window with apprehension. Better one player should sit out. Better still, the library should fit the number and type of instruments.

Larger Forms

Brahms wrote two fine string sextets, and there are many compositions for six or more players, some of them very effective. More than five players in the home causes space and logistics difficulties. (There is problem in heating water for six or more cups of tea for refreshments afterwards, for example.) Compositions for more than five players are best relegated to the chamber music societies unless the host can provide a large room and a high-capacity teapot.

Duos with Piano

There is a wealth of sonata literature for piano and strings. The piano-violin sonatas of Mozart and Beethoven are good training for quartet players. Beethoven described his 10 as sonatas for pianoforte with violin accompaniment. Since the pianist has most of the notes, it is best to leave the choice of music to him. The violinist need not worry about making himself heard; the quality of the sound assures this if he plays naturally. Many composers, from

Beethoven on, wrote fine sonatas for cello and piano. Much of the sonata literature for viola and piano is transcriptions, but the two wonderful Brahms sonatas of his Op. 120 were published to be played either by B♭ clarinet or viola, and both versions are magnificent. Even so, the clarinet version sounds better, because it was this instrument Brahms had in mind as he wrote. The last composition of Dmitry Shostakovich was a sonata for piano and viola.

A Key Note

In the best-forgotten origins of the Ill Tempered Strings, quartets with more than three sharps or flats were passed over by common consent as too difficult, and passages such as the F♯ major (six sharps) *Largo* of Haydn, Op. 76, No. 5, or the B (five sharps) in the *Adagio* of Op. 76, No. 6, were met with collective groans. With experience, however, no key signature daunted the players. A string instrument player becomes used to the minute adjustments in finger positions required to play in tune, guided by his ear. A violin player will be able to play as much in tune on a 3/4-size fiddle or a viola as he does on his usual instrument—or at least no worse—instantly. The relationship of key signature and tonic key is tabulated:

Sharps	0	1	2	3	4	5	6	7	0	0	0	0	0	0	0
Flats	0	0	0	0	0	0	0	0	1	2	3	4	5	6	7
Major	C	G	D	A	E	B	F♯	C♯	F	B♭	E♭	A♭	D♭	G♭	C♭
Minor	a	e	b	f♯	c♯	g♯	d♯	a♯	d	g	c	f	b♭	e♭	a♭

The piano is a well-tempered instrument, which manages all keys by compromise to make close ones identical. Thus C = B♯, C♯ = D♭, D♯ = E♭, E = F♭, F = E♯, F♯ = G♭, G♯ = A♭, A♯ = B♭, B = C♭. These notes are not the same on a violin, but they are called enharmonics on the piano. On a piano, then, the C♯ major scale (with seven sharps) is identical with the D♭ major scale (five flats), and the C♭ major scale (seven flats) uses the same keys as the B major scale (five sharps). (The International edition of the Dvořák *Viola Quintet*, Op. 97, provides an alternative for several bars of the slow movement in A♭ minor for the first violin, showing this in G♯ minor. It is easier, of course, to read and play.)

One can imbibe a lot of music theory by playing and working out relationships on a piano keyboard. (It is not necessary to be able to play the piano, only to know where the notes are.) Some players may have been exposed to music theory during their initial training. Others may not. Those who are interested can find plenty of formal instruction or learn by themselves. The tonic key — the key in which a composition begins and, usually, ends — has been mentioned throughout as a guide for the number of sharps or flats employed.

Inexorable Time

An occasional sour note — a "clinker," to use the technical term — is like an air bubble in a flow of liquid. It is a disturbance, but the flow continues. Losing the beat by one of the players may choke off the flow. The cacophony that results may cause the players to stop, but most players learn how to get back in after they have been out of rhythm. Amateurs sometimes refer to "record speed," meaning by this the tempo of professionals as heard in recordings. The reference usually accompanies a statement that they intend to play it slower in order to handle the notes. In most instances, they start slower, but the music dictates that they end up very close to "record speed." Directions such as *"Andante, Adagio, Lento, Allegro, Presto"* and so on are vague. These have to be interpreted along with time signatures, such as 2/4, 6/8, 3/4 and 4/4. Is a 4/4 *Allegro* faster than a cut-time 4/4 *Andante*? Is a 6/8 *Presto* slower than a 2/4 *Presto*?

A music dictionary often is frustrating. The definition of *Andantino* in my pocket dictionary is that it usually means slower than *Andante*, but sometimes means faster. Beethoven was an early enthusiast for use of Maelzel metronome markings; then he found later that he disagreed with the numbers he had assigned. (Johann Nepomuk Maelzel, 1772–1838, produced a clockwork metronome in 1816.) It has been seen that Beethoven gave very elaborate directions on speed and mood. No matter; however the players start out, they usually end up at about the right speed. The music dictates it.

It is sometimes advantageous for a player to change his count during a movement. A 6/8 *Presto* for example can be interpreted often as slower than a 2/4 *Presto,* and it may be useful to count it both ways in different sections of one movement, depending on how the part is laid out. A 2/4 *Andante* can often be counted as 4/8 (or "1—and 2—and") in many theme and variations movements, switching to 6/8 when triplet or sextuplet figures are encountered.

Dynamics

The differences between *piano* and *forte* are relative and arguable (and much argued). The universal truth is that every player in an amateur quartet knows that the other three are playing *fortes* too loud and *pianos* very much too loud. First fiddles are frequently egregious offenders on dynamics. This dear fellow is so busy counting, trying to articulate chromatic passages at *Prestissimo* tempo and stretching desperately for the correct note—or even one that harmonizes with it—on the high reaches of his E string, that he often cannot pay attention to changes from *ff* to *pp*. He compromises on a resolute *mf*. The other players, with fewer high-risk problems in their parts, have no charity. The middle voices of the quartet, fearful their contributions might not be recognized, tend to be overly assertive when playing accompaniment figures. Dynamic range, or—more accurately—its absence, provides a major source of ill temper in an amateur string quartet. Until the players are able to play in time and in tune, there is no profit in recriminations about volume.

Amateur string players usually feel they have to play louder than usual when they play with piano. Tone and musicality suffer. There is no doubt that the piano can produce louder sounds, but the fiddle player does not hear himself accurately—a blessing for many of us. The quality of string instrument tone is different from that of the piano. The fiddle players may not believe they project, but they do. They do.

XIV. The High-Strung Amateur String Quartet Player

O Tempora, O Mores

The death of domestic music-making is bemoaned by many writers on music, who point out that entertainment in the home is available on radio, recordings and television. This, they claim, has changed leisure activities for the masses from the active production of music to passive consumption of it. There was a time when the cultivated persons in a community played or sang at home, when piano four-hand arrangements of symphonies and violin duets were popular. This was a time, however, when the majority of men worked six days each week — and the women, seven. Only the monied classes enjoyed much leisure.

Undoubtedly, some of those who labored many hours each week and their families passed some of their leisure hours with music. Judging from the availability of music from publishers for combinations such as two violins and piano, music-making in the home seems to have decreased as compared with generations ago. Whether or not the proportion of amateur musicians in our population has decreased is a question we leave to social historians. One may propose that the availability of easy transportation has led to a replacement of house music by the thousands of amateur bands, orchestras and choral groups that exist — that small groups have been replaced by large.

The great virtue of small groups, one player or singer to a part, is lost in large ones. Choral groups and orchestras include people who have solo turns. There is no difficulty in recruiting competent solo singers, oboists or horns. Selectivity often needs be compromised in staffing the choruses and the string sections. The principals in each large section of an amateur group follow the conductor; the others do so to varying degrees, but the further back in the section the greater reliance on the neighboring musician. Given enough rehearsal, the back row musicians can learn their entrances and simulate playing during the technically-difficult passages. They lack the incentive to improve in technique and musicianship that comes from the exposure of one person per part. Although the prevalence of music in the home may have decreased, it has never disappeared. The growth in popularity of concert and recorded performances of chamber music in the past decades may have stimulated interest in amateur chamber music. From the standpoint of those of us who continually need to recruit new quartet players, this has provided encouragement.

The Closet Musician

"I used to play the trumpet [or whatever] but I haven't picked it up in years." This is a common statement of people who learn that we play in a quartet. Often, their instrument lies neglected in a closet or attic. The closet musician tells, rather ruefully, that he had been a "pretty good player" and wishes he had "stayed with it." Few of them ever quit for lack of ability, but other pressures made them stop playing. It is not a wasted experience. Having more or less learned the elements of music in some form, they may become more appreciative audiences for professional musicians and encourage their children to learn music. It is better to have played and discarded an instrument than never to have tried at all.

The Parental Piano

Many a home contains a piano, sometimes a glorious piece of furniture that one of the children *used* to play: mute testimony to the status of the householder as a member of the cultured classes. Arthur Rubinstein wrote that his family knew he was a prodigy when he climbed to the piano at age three and played his sister's lesson assignment first with all the mistakes she made, then the way her teacher played it. Most children start lessons with visions of having such a near-miraculous ability to play the instrument, but they are discouraged by all the work needed to get by unscathed by the teacher at their next lesson. Many persist with piano lessons for a year or two or five, until a weary parent tires of fighting the daily battle over practice.

The more talented piano students may play in school assemblies and with the school orchestra, but the number of potential pianists diminishes with time until there are relatively few in high schools. As young adults, they may move miles from the parental piano, living in quarters where a piano would be an intrusion on the peace of the neighbors. When they sit at the instrument again, mind instructs fingers, but fingers do not obey. The availability of electronic keyboards could lead to a continuity of practice for young adults with motivation. One of the great virtues of the piano is that it is complete in itself, providing melody, harmony, dynamics and rhythm. The pianist can play alone from a vast literature. Professional pianists can be assured of discerning audiences of amateur pianists for recitals of the literature. The amateur pianist can play for his own enjoyment, but doing this regularly requires a relatively high degree of self-discipline and enough ability to avoid frustration at the results of his efforts.

The independence of the piano is both a virtue and a detriment. Some pianists may derive ego-satisfaction from their solitary efforts, but others feel a social need to interact. The gregarious pianist may find satisfaction in playing with singers or playing four-hand literature with other pianists. (One may note that the ACMP has a listing for pianists who like four-hand arrangements.) Relatively few pianists have discovered the pleasures of piano-violin sonatas, trios, etc., where the piano is a partner and not an accompanying instrument.

The Voice

Singing is a musical activity open to most people. The requirements are that they can carry a tune and have, or can develop, a sense of rhythm. The instrument is always available, but its quality varies over an enormous range. No amount of money can buy a good voice. What one has may be trained, but a trained crow cannot sound like a nightingale. On the other hand, a good voice unaccompanied by intelligence, training and sensibility is like a Stradivari violin in the hands of a beginner. Where the voice is adequate, amateur singers can make music together in school and church choirs and in organizations like the Society for Preservation and Encouragement of Barbershop Singing in America, the Sweet Adelines and the Dapper Dans. Amateur singers may join together to sing madrigals or folk songs. The medium and the music are much different than for string quartet players, but the spirit is the same.

Wind Instruments

Band instruments are easier to learn than the violin, viola and cello. The sounds produced by beginners usually are less unpleasant and invariably are louder than for us with our wooden boxes. The loudness, especially, makes them attractive to school children. There is no problem getting recruits to play trumpet, trombone, clarinets, flutes, saxophones and drums for a school band. Beginners can look forward to the thrill of donning Graustarkian guard costumes and marching in parades and at athletic events. The best of each section are recruited for the few positions needed in the school orchestra. After high school, the better players among those that go on to college can play in university bands and orchestras.

The wind instrument players have a respectable repertory for small combinations where each player has his own part: chamber music. Their most difficult problem is finding a place to play. There is much music for brass choir or a woodwind octet that is very attractive, but one needs a home isolated from neighbors, and family members with great forebearance, to arrange house music with the wind instrument combinations. Salvation Army bands use the proper chamber for wind instrument players: none at all. The great classical composers wrote divertimenti for wind instruments which were intended to be played outdoors in garden parties. The wind players can arrange to play jazz together if they are good enough musicians to improvise and they can arrange a place to play. The attrition rate is such that band instruments are always available in classified advertisements, but it is likely that most instruments are stored away in the closet to that day when time is available to restore the desiccated instrument pads and resume playing. It rarely arrives.

Amplified Instruments

Electronic amplification of music has allowed small groups of musicians to fill stadiums seating 50,000 listeners with sound. The guitar, long used as accompaniment in folk music, a solo instrument and, in Boccherini quintets, a participant in chamber music, has been amplified to a raucous voice in modern music. (This has engendered the neologism "acoustic guitar" for the old and civilized version of the instrument.) One person equipped with any instrument, even an electronic violin, and amplifiers and loudspeakers is more than sufficient to drown out any attempt at civilized conversation in a bar and lounge. Most people must find this entertaining because it is so prevalent, but it motivates some of us traveling curmudgeons to head for a liquor store near our hotel so that we can carry on relaxed conversation with our friends in the quiet ambiance of our hotel rooms.

Electronic instuments and amplification for conventional instruments and keyboards interfaced with computers are available. The latter can facilitate the production of musical manuscripts. Other marvels of technology enable the unmusical to produce musical sounds, but fortunately they seem to tire of this activity quickly. It is paradoxical that the amount spent on electronic equipment for reproducing sound seems to be the greatest for people with the least interest in music.

With Strings Attached

Learning to play a violin, viola or cello is not easy. It requires a good ear and the development of a high order of neuromuscular coordination. Explaining the career of a child prodigy on the violin whose playing deteriorated in his early adult years, a music educator said, "What a pity that he found a teacher who told him that playing the

violin is hard." Becoming good enough to make a living at playing requires a prodigious amount of natural ability, excellent training,
charisma and luck. There are more excellent instrumentalists than there
are jobs for them. It is a very competitive occupation where the competition forces down the price. The financial rewards for playing string
instruments exceedingly well do not come close to the talent, effort and
money expended to reach that status. Only a relative few, distinguished
by impeccable technique and unique persona and blessed with luck,
can become wealthy and famous. The choirs of string players needed
in orchestras provide work for some of the best of the professionals, who
supplement their income by teaching and pick-up jobs.

The Well-Schooled Fiddler

Lessons on violin or cello begin in childhod for most people. The
fortunate ones begin when they are too young for school so that the fine
muscle skills needed can become part of their development. Private
preschool lessons usually derive from some evidence of precociousness
in the child and a family background in music. Group lessons for
preschool children became popular with the Suzuki method. More
children get first lessons at age nine or later in school. Whether or not
children are offered and accept training in the playing of violin or cello
depends heavily on family cultural values. Sometimes a child is dissatis-
fied with piano lessons and asks to be given lessons on a more linear instrument. The child cellist may elect that instrument to avoid com-
peting with a family member who plays the violin or who expresses a
preference for its sound. School children may be offered lessons on viola
or cello if these instruments are needed for school orchestras. Increas-
ingly, one meets people who started playing viola from lessons in
school, although most viola players begin as violinists.

Unless there is exposure to the wonderful literature of chamber
music through family or friends, the schoolchild fiddler is exposed to
music only as orchestral compositions and recital pieces. Private lessons
extend from études to concerti. Once free from the obligations of the
school orchestra and regular lessons, the student may be motivated to
join one or more of the ubiquitous amateur symphony orchestras in his

locality. Some cannot commit the time to regular rehearsals, and they practice at irregular intervals at home. They play through the solo parts of concerti and sonatas, skipping the virtuoso passages and playing with an unconscionable amount of rubato in most of what remains. Fortunately, they cannot hear themselves as others do. Unlike the self-sufficient pianist, the player of a bowed string instrument needs other players to make music and improve his technique. The fiddler who plays with just one other or a pianist to work through duos benefits from the experience in having direction and motivation for practice in ensemble. The eventual discovery of the string quartet literature provides motivation for a lifetime of study.

The Adult Neophyte

More and more, one meets people who began playing the violin, viola or cello as adults. One woman we know began college as a piano major and fell in love with the cello, required as a secondary instrument. A man, having abandoned piano lessons in his boyhood, decided to take viola lessons many years later when he was established as a research scientist so that he could become an amateur chamber music player. Some adults are motivated to become string-instrument players after their marriage to players. The adult beginners have neither the capacity nor the desire to be virtuosi on their instruments, but most of them reach a level of competence.

The Amateur Professional

What do professional string-instrument players do for recreation? Play string quartets, of course. An acquaintance invited me one day to his home for a quartet session he had arranged with his colleagues, all players in a professional symphony orchestra. The quartets were set up for early afternoon, because three of the players had professional work later in the day. They had not played together before, but the contrast with most amateurs was remarkable. They played most of the notes, and they played all of the music. Except in very few spots, their feet did not move; counting took place between their ears. They stopped only a couple of times, quickly discovered their problem and continued. They observed the dynamics markings and adjusted to each other in this and in rhythm through unspoken signals. This amateur was surprised to find he had much greater familiarity with the music they played than the professionals did. One player said that the chance to play chamber music made playing in an orchestra worthwhile. It was a glorious experience for an auditor who had required years to be able to play these works tolerably. These professional musicians were playing string quartets for the love of it; their faces showed it and the music they produced demonstrated it. They were—for this day—highly qualified amateurs. We have not enjoyed listening to any famous professional string quartet more.

The Professional Amateur

We occasionally meet the amateur bowed instrument players who might have become professionals but dropped out of the race to enter a less competitive and demanding profession, brain surgery, say, or theoretical chemistry. Some of these can be found in the concertmaster's or viola or cello principal's chairs in amateur orchestras. Some supplement their family income by giving lessons. These are some of the people in the ACMP Directory who list themselves as Vl- or Vla- or Vc-Pro. They are professional musicians but, either by accident or choice, they are not professional players. They constitute the top rank of amateur chamber music players. When the tolerance gained by teaching extends to playing quartets with their less gifted friends, they raise the level of the rest of us.

The Never-Could-Be-Professional

Here we have the largest group of amateur chamber music players, those of us whose musicality was not developed early enough, whose industry exceeds our artistry, whose love for playing is not approached by our aptitude. We have not passed the peak of our playing ability; we spend our years struggling up the mountain, never looking down at the base camp. Playing chamber music with our peers provides a nearly perfect recreation activity. It can be arranged at any mutually convenient time, it is social, it provides physical and mental exercise, it has continual personal goals and requires such concentration that all other concerns and worries are swept away.

A View to the Future

We take the assumption that amateur fiddle players and their teachers know about the attractions of chamber music, but the premise, alas, is not correct in most instances. (We have the altruistic hope that this book will help arouse interest among instrumentalists in general, and the self-serving one that it will provide more prospects for companionship in our own chamber music activities.) Few string instrument teachers, either in schools or as private teachers of children, seem to expose their students to chamber music. A great opportunity is lost. We believe that chamber music should be a primary means for teaching all musicians. Playing music where each player has a part which must interact with the others provides a stimulus for study that can never be realized in a string section of an orchestra. Unlike the orchestral, chamber music provides no hiding place for the stringed-instrument player. People who have played in amateur orchestra string sections for years, carried along by other players, discover much greater need for concentration when they first try sight-reading chamber music with one or more other players. Dramatic improvement in their playing is often the response to the stimulus they get from this experience. Many of the readers of this work may infer that the author is preaching to the already converted. We admit this; however, we have the further expectation of recruiting missionaries to our cause.

Appendix. The Interpretation of Musical Terms

There is no intention here of providing a glossary or a dictionary. Instead we offer an idiosyncratic survey of some words encountered during quartet playing where heated discussion damaged the harmony of the players.

Accelerando, Accelerato. Accelerate the tempo to a rousing finish or to reach a new, faster tempo. This is a mess unless the lower strings follow the first violin, who should lead with exaggerated body language.

Adagio. Slower than *Andante* and faster than *Largo*; however, time signature, e.g., cut-time, and modifiers such as *più, meno, molto,* etc., vitiate the meaning.

Affettuoso. Tenderly, with great feeling.

Allargando. Becoming gradually and markedly slower.

Alto clef. Same as viola clef, which see.

Appoggiatura. Grace note, in classical music; usually played borrowing from time of succeeding note, especially if written without a line through the stem.

Arco. With the bow, cancelling *pizzicato.*

Assai. Very; *not* a cognate of French *assez.*

Assez. Enough, quite.

Attacca. Begin a section without stopping, after completing a previous movement or section.

Audience, Auditors. A distraction for an amateur string quartet.

Baroque. In music, it describes the style from about 1600 to about 1750; the music and instrumentation of Frescobaldi, Bach, Handel, Vivaldi, Corelli, et al. A baroque violin or cello is one set up as in that period, using a flatter neck angle, shorter fingerboard and gut strings. "Authentic performances" using antique or modern versions of baroque instruments have resurrected the clatter of harpsichords in concert halls.

Bariolage. An effect produced in extended passages by alternating the same notes on adjacent strings, taking advantage of the different qualities of the strings. The effect is wretched if the alternated notes differ in pitch by microtones.

Bratsche. German for viola, homonym for Italian *braccia* (arm) as in *viola di braccia,* arm viol.

Calando. Growing softer, often slower, but the leader should not slow unless all the players know the definition.

Cello. 1. Instrument of violin family (formally known as the violoncello), tuned an octave lower than the viola. 2. Player on the instrument.

Classical. 1. Music written in sonata form as chamber music and symphonies, from Haydn about 1750 to late-period Beethoven about 1820, succeeding baroque and merging into romantic. 2. What used to be "long-hair music" before popular musicians boycotted barbers.

Clef. 1. Indication where note is located on staff. 2. French for key. Clefs in string quartets are treble for the violins, viola (or alto) and treble for the viola, and bass, tenor, treble and "false treble" for the cello. False treble for the cello is intended to be played an octave lower than it is written, and many cellists panic.

Dynamics. The notation in music scores of variations in loudness (degrees of *forte*) and softness (degrees of *piano*), *crescendos* and *diminuendos*. The observance of these niceties is the last stage in the development of a competent amateur chamber music player. Although poor dynamics is less disruptive than loss of the beat or playing out of tune, it is the greatest source of ill temper in an amateur quartet session.

Editor. Person who put in fingerings and, often, dynamics markings and bowings according to the fashion of his day. The influence of editors, as has been alleged for the electorate in Chicago, remains long after their deaths.

Espressione. Expressively, with vibrato and feeling.

Flageolet. Fingered harmonics, appropriately named after a whistle-like flute.

Flautando, Flautato. Playing near the fingerboard to obtain a fluty sound.

Forte. Strong or loud; what everyone else is playing when you are following the direction to play *piano*.

G.P. Grand pause, an indication that all players should observe *and count* a rest. If anyone is playing, it is a good place to gather forces.

Largo. Slow and stately.

Legato. Tied together in one bow.

Lento. Slow.

L'istesso tempo. The same speed as immediately preceding, although note values and time signature are changed.

Lunga pausa. Long pause, usually at end of section.

M.M. *M*aezel's *M*etronome marking, in beats per minute.

Mancando. Dying away, see *Morendo.*

Marcato. Marked, emphasized. distinct.

Meno. Less.

Mesto. Sad.

Minuet. An old dance in 3/4 time, usually the second or third movement of a quartet. It includes a *Trio*, which contrasts with it. The minuet is played with repeats before playing the *Trio* and without afterwards. People with no taste like to slow the last few measures at the end. The term, *Menuetto,* is a corruption used by editors of the Italian *Minuetto* from the German *Menuett.*

Moderato. Moderately.

Molto. Much, very.

Morendo. Dying away, getting softer.

Moto. Motion, tempo. Most often used as *con moto,* with movement. Nearly as often used in *Andante con moto,* which could be translated literally as "moving along with movement." So much for the precision of musical directions.

Piano. 1. Softly; volume of sound obtained by drawing bow on strings without trying to play either loudly or very softly. 2. The instrument known formally as a pianoforte.

Più. More.

Pizzicato. Direction to pluck strings, leaving the bow in hand at the ready.

Poco. Somewhat.

Prestissimo. As fast as the best player in the quartet can play.

Presto. As fast as three of the players in the quartet can play.

Rinforzando, Rfz. Sudden increase in emphasis, louder and broader vibrato.

Romantic. Music from about the Beethoven of the late quartets to about the First World War. Although many classical forms were retained, the conventions were stretched.

Semplice. Unadorned, little or no vibrato.

Senza. Without, as in *Senza sordino,* without mute.

Sforzando, Sf, Sfz. With sudden emphasis. Use more bow.

Soggetti. Subjects or themes, as in *Fuga à dué soggetti* (a fugue with two themes).

Sopra una corda. To be played on one string, allowing for the same tone color and, where appropriate, some discrete slides, e.g., in the first violin part of the *Trio* of Haydn, Op. 33, No. 2.

String quartet. 1. Music written for two violins, viola and cello. 2. The players. 3. The group in an orchestra.

Stringendo. Pressing the tempo suddenly; pronounced as in "stringent" and cognate to it. Nothing to do with "string." See *Accelerando*.

Subito. Right away, as in *Attacca subito*.

Tanto. Too much; invariably used in *non tanto*, not too much.

Trio. 1. A group of three players. 2. A composition for three players. 3. The contrasting middle part of a minuet.

Trio sonata. Baroque composition for four instruments in three parts, usually two treble instruments, a keyboard and a bass instrument (cello, double bass or bassoon) reinforcing a harpsichord bass line.

Troppo. See *Tanto*.

Vif. Lively.

Viol. A bowed string instrument of Baroque era, superseded by violin family. The doublebass is a vestige still in use.

Viola. 1. Instrument of the violin family, usually from 38 to 43 cm. in back length and tuned a fifth lower than the violin—i.e., A, D, G, C. 2. Person who plays the instrument.

Viola clef. Alto clef, a C clef where middle C is the middle line of the staff, the upper two lines are the lower two lines of the treble clef, and lower two lines are the top two lines of the bass clef.

Viole. French for viola or viol.

Violin. 1. Musical (when played well) instrument, usually 355 mm. in back length for full size. 2. Person who plays the instrument, varying considerably in back length and other dimensions.

Violist. 1. Person who plays the viola. 2. A player on a viol.

Violon. French for violin.

Violoncello. 1. Literally, small violone; see *Cello*. 2. A pretentious way of naming a cello.

Violone. Variously, a bass viol, a double bass, or a cello.

Vivace. Lively, not to be confused with *Prestissimo*.

Voice. In quartets; instruments, as in "middle voice" for second violin or viola.

Zingara. Gypsy.

Index